HÖLDERLIN'S HYMN
"REMEMBRANCE"

Studies in Continental Thought

JOHN SALLIS, EDITOR

Martin Heidegger

HÖLDERLIN'S HYMN "REMEMBRANCE"

Translated by

William McNeill and Julia Ireland

Indiana University Press

This book is a publication of

Indiana University Press
Office of Scholarly Publishing
Herman B Wells Library 350
1320 East 10th Street
Bloomington, Indiana 47405 USA

iupress.indiana.edu

Published in German as Martin Heidegger,
Gesamtausgabe 52: Hölderlins Hymne "Andenken"
© 1992 by Vittorio Klostermann, Frankfurt am Main

English translation © 2018 by Indiana University Press

The paper used in this publication meets the minimum requirements of the
American National Standard for Information Sciences—Permanence of Paper for
Printed Library Materials, ANSI Z39.48-1992.

Manufactured in the United States of America

Cataloging information is available from the Library of Congress.

ISBN 978-0-253-03581-3 (hdbk.)
ISBN 978-0-253-03587-5 (web PDF)

1   2   3   4   5   23   22   21   20   19   18

Contents

APPENDIX

TRANSLATORS' FOREWORD

The present volume makes available in English the second of three lecture courses that Heidegger devoted to the poetry of Friedrich Hölderlin at the University of Freiburg. The first, on Hölderlin's hymns "Germania" and "The Rhine," was given in the winter semester of 1934–1935;[1] the course on the hymn "Remembrance" was presented seven years later, in the winter of semester 1941–1942;[2] and the third, on the hymn "The Ister," took place the following semester, in the summer semester of 1942.[3] The special significance of this particular lecture course on "Remembrance" for Heidegger is indicated by a number of considerations. In the fall of 1941, Heidegger's plan was to provide interpretations (more precisely, a series of "pointers" or "remarks," as he preferred to call them) of five of Hölderlin's poems, which he listed in order as "Remembrance," "The Ister," "The Titans," "Mnemosyne," and "Ripe, bathed in fire . . ."[4] In a note from September 1941, reproduced as the appendix to this volume, he explicitly noted that "The interpretation of 'Remembrance' provides the foundation and orientation, and the perspectives for all that follows." While in fact Heidegger only managed to give detailed interpretations of the first two poems (the others being touched upon or referred to in passing, but without detailed exegesis), the foundational role of "Remembrance" for the interpretation of all the remaining hymns, including the extensive interpretation of "The Ister" in the following semester, is thereby indicated.[5]

---

1 *Hölderlins Hymnen "Germanien" und "Der Rhein."* Gesamtausgabe Band 39. Frankfurt: Klostermann, 1980. Third edition, 1999. Translated as *Hölderlin's Hymns "Germania" and "The Rhine"* by William McNeill and Julia Ireland. Bloomington: Indiana University Press, 2014.

2 *Hölderlins Hymne "Andenken."* Gesamtausgabe Band 52. Frankfurt: Klostermann, 1982. Second edition, 1992.

3 *Hölderlins Hymne "Der Ister."* Gesamtausgabe Band 53. Frankfurt: Klostermann, 1984. Second edition, 1993. Translated as *Hölderlin's Hymn "The Ister"* by William McNeill and Julia Davis. Bloomington: Indiana University Press, 1996.

4 See the Preliminary Considerations in the present volume.

5 Other important texts that indicate the pivotal role of "Remembrance" include the 1936 essay "*Hölderlin und das Wesen der Dichtung*" ("Hölderlin and the Essence of Poetry"), in *Erläuterungen zu Hölderlins Dichtung.* Frankfurt: Klostermann, 1951, 31–45. Translated as *Elucidations of Hölderlin's Poetry* by Keith Hoeller. Amherst, New York: Humanity Books,

Furthermore, of all four hymns that Heidegger lectured on in his three major lecture courses ("Germania," "The Rhine," "Remembrance," and "The Ister"), "Remembrance" is the only one that he chose to publish a commentary on, albeit in abbreviated form, during his lifetime.[6] It is also the poem that Heidegger felt most compelled to repeatedly revisit and reinterpret. In particular, it is of central importance for the final lecture course that Heidegger gave, the course "What Is Called Thinking?" delivered at the University of Freiburg in 1951–1952.[7]

As noted in our forewords to the translations of the other lecture courses, translating Heidegger's interpretations of Hölderlin presents special challenges, not least that of rendering Hölderlin's poetry into English. As with previous volumes, our translation cites the original German poetry alongside the English, and tries to adapt our translations of the poetry to the intricacies and nuances of Heidegger's readings. Although the translations offered here are our own, we have consulted and benefited from the existing translations of Hölderlin by Michael Hamburger, adopting his solutions in particular instances. Readers may wish to examine Hamburger's translations for alternative renditions of the poetry.[8]

As the lecture course explains, remembrance (in German, *Andenken*), is a particular kind of thinking (*Denken*), a "commemorative thinking" that "must remain unknown to every doctrine of thinking hitherto."[9] Its meaning is inseparable from the structure of greeting poetized in the hymn, from the nature of holidays (*Feiertage*, literally: days of celebration) and festivity, and from the essence of destiny and history and the task, for the Germans, of finding and appropriating what is their own in relation to the Greek beginning of Western thinking. This task would be taken up and further developed in Heidegger's lecture course on "The Ister" that directly followed.

2000, 51–65; and the 1939 reflections *"Andenken" und "Mnemosyne,"* in *Zu Hölderlin. Griechenlandsreisen.* Gesamtausgabe Band 75. Frankfurt: Klostermann, 2000, 3–32.

6 Heidegger's essay *"Andenken"* was first published in the *Tübinger Gedenkschrift zum hundersten Todestag Hölderlins* [Tübingen Memorial Text on the Hundredth Anniversary of Hölderlin's Death]. Tübingen: J.C.B. Mohr, 1943. It was subsequently included in the collection of Heidegger's essays on Hölderlin, *Erläuterungen zu Hölderlins Dichtung.* Frankfurt: Klostermann, 1951, 75–143. Translated as *Elucidations of Hölderlin's Poetry* by Keith Hoeller. Amherst, NY: Humanity Books, 2000, 101–173. The published essay *"Andenken"* represents a substantially condensed and revised interpretation that occasionally borrows from the lecture course.

7 *Was Heißt Denken?* Tübingen: Niemeyer, 1954. Translated as *What Is Called Thinking?* by J. Glenn Gray. New York: Harper & Row, 1968.

8 See Michael Hamburger, *Friedrich Hölderlin: Selected Poems and Fragments.* Penguin Classics Edition. London: Penguin Books, 1998.

9 See §65. *The Founding of the Coming Holy in the Word.*

References to Hölderlin are to the von Hellingrath edition used by Heidegger. Translators' notes are indicated in square brackets and provided at the end of the volume. The German text shows a number of inconsistencies of style and typography; generally, we have reproduced these in our translation, as it remains unclear whether they are found in Heidegger's manuscript or were introduced inadvertently in the editing process. For example, the German word for *memory* appears in three different variations: In the first citing of the hymn, it appears as *Gedächtniß* (GA 52, 21); in section 63, as *Gedächtniss* (187); and in section 64 as *Gedächtnis* (192). For details of the original manuscript and principles of editing for the German volume, see the editor's epilogue. German–English and English–German glossaries indicating the translation of key terms are also provided.

The translators would like to thank Ian Alexander Moore and Christopher Turner, graduate students at DePaul University, who reviewed early drafts of the translation and made numerous suggestions for improvement. Julia Ireland would like to thank Lara Mehling of Whitman College for her translation help in generating a first draft of the first sections of the lecture course. William McNeill would like to thank DePaul University for a University Research Council grant that funded the review of the translation, as well as the College of Liberal Arts and Social Sciences for a summer research grant that enabled the completion of this project. Julia Ireland would like to thank Whitman College for the the Louis B. Perry Research Grant that supported work on the translation, and the Alexander von Humboldt Foundation that enabled her to review Heidegger's original manuscripts at the Deutsches Literaturarchiv in Marbach am Neckar, Germany.

HÖLDERLIN'S HYMN
"REMEMBRANCE"

Preliminary Considerations

Preparation for Hearing the Word
of the Poetizing

The lecture course is only a pointing.

This lecture course would like to draw attention to a few of Hölderlin's poems. To this end, the following poems have been selected:

> Remembrance, IV, 61ff.[1]
> The Ister, IV, 220ff.
> The Titans, IV, 208ff. (also 215ff.)
> Mnemosyne, IV, 225f.
> Ripe, bathed in fire . . . , IV, 71.

A few things ought to be said about the selection of these poems, and likewise concerning that toward which our thinking is to be steered. This calls for preliminary considerations that seemingly already anticipate what is essential. Yet in truth, prefaces readily stray into vacuousness because they have yet to hear the word of the poetizing. Everything hinges on that alone. If at some point we have become hearers, however, then extensive "introductions" easily become a hindrance.

If at some point we have become hearers—getting to that point is admittedly a long path. To follow this path means to leave behind much that is habitual and supposedly obvious; it means to renounce hasty goals and trivial hopes. Yet because we break with what we are accustomed to with the greatest difficulty, seeing that we also accommodate within it what we are unaccustomed to; because, without our knowing it, we everywhere have at the ready what we are most accustomed to as the safety net for everything, we must here first abandon the customary relationship to "works" of poetry. We must forthwith make ourselves ready for another path. For this it is necessary already at the beginning of this path to awaken a disposition toward Hölderlin's word, one in which we may perhaps one day indeed become hearers of this word. Yet such preparation is of necessity forced

---

1 Concerning the Norbert von Hellingrath edition of Hölderlin's works cited throughout, see pp. 12–13.

to take the often unfruitful form of mere rejection. We thereby state what the lecture course does not intend. Through this, we indirectly make clear a few things concerning that which it does intend.

§1. What the lecture course does not intend. On literary-historiographical research and the arbitrary interpretation of poetry

The lecture course does not intend to compete with "literary-historiographical" research into Hölderlin's "life and works" in presenting the "correct" or even the "definitive" Hölderlin, as though he were a specimen to be worked on by natural science. The historian indeed likes to persist in the peculiar view that a historical life, a historical process, a historical deed, is "correctly" grasped only if and when the process, the life, or the work is in each case explained in terms of the "conditions of its time period" and placed into that context. To what extent is this illuminating and widely acknowledged ideal of historiographical knowledge peculiar? What is peculiar about this view is that it consists in the belief that the "milieu" of the period presents itself to the historian as it is in itself and of its own accord. He need only place the work to be explained within the relevant "time period" and into the "circumstances" that the period gives rise to so that, on the basis of tracing it back to its conditions, the work would stand there independently and objectively as a historiographical object.

Yet that past era to which the work belongs is, to be sure, just as closed off and just as evident for historiographical apprehension as is the work to be explained. Why should the historical conditions be historiographically more accessible than what is historically conditioned? The appeal to the conditions and facts of the time period that are supposed to explain something is misguided; for these conditions of the time period are just as in need of explanation as what they supposedly situate and condition, such as a work.

Perhaps the interpretation of a work can even say something more readily about the period in which it arose and about the "conditions" of its time than these conditions can say about the work. Yet how, then, should the work be comprehended, assuming that the whole heap of "literary-historiographical facts" surely tells us something only when those "facts" are for their part also already adequately interpreted? Literary-historiographical research, indeed all historiography and every science, stands under conditions that it itself can so little master that it can never grasp, let alone ground, these conditions by means of its own cognitive resources.

Do such considerations invalidate literary-historiographical research? No. Within its limits, such research remains indispensable. Within these limits it secures the reliability and editions of works, and it investigates the life-history of poets and authors.

Yet even this seemingly wholly extraneous and technical activity always already operates on the basis of certain representations concerning "poetry," poets, works, artworks, art, language, world, history, and so forth. It is for this reason that even the smallest genuine contribution to research— when it keeps its eye on what is essential—is never possible as a merely technical accomplishment. Literary-historiographical research leads itself astray, however, and, like all historiography, falls prey to vanity if it presumes that with its style of research it could ever disclose the truth of history.

History opens itself only to history. Only the poet who himself founds history lets us recognize what poetry is and perhaps must be. Only the thinker who grounds history brings thinkers of the past to speak. Only builders engaged in the work of building history show us its corridors. Historiography, in its limping along behind, only gives rise to the vanity of a prodigious scholarship and contributes at most to confusing our sense for history.

What history is, however, we can perhaps learn to intimate at certain junctures in this lecture course. The lecture course does not pursue any literary-historiographical aims. It therefore also renounces any claim to make us aware of the "historiographically correct" "Hölderlin." And perhaps this renunciation is indeed not as significant as it may at first appear.

Yet does not this renunciation in fact have troublesome consequences? If we are not aiming to portray the "historiographically correct" Hölderlin, indeed if there may not even "be" such a thing, is not everything then left to whim? Cannot everyone, then, according to taste and mood and need read into and read out of the poet whatever happens to occur to them at the time? Does not the concern to present the objectively real version of Hölderlin's work in a manner that is correct in terms of literary historiography then have the advantage over the sweeping arbitrariness of even the most inspired interpretation?

Yet this kind of interpretation and that kind of research are not at all opposed to each other. Rather, they correspond to each other. It is only if one knows no alternative to literary-historiographical research that every other kind of undertaking becomes branded as arbitrary interpretation. Only when one becomes fixated on such interpretation does every attempt to make accessible the historical essence of Hölderlin's poetry get set on equal footing with literary-historiographical objectification and measured according to its standards. Both, literary-historiographical research and gratuitous interpretation, fall equally short in their knowledge of what they do and what they are capable of, and under which laws they stand.

We renounce the claim to uncover the historiographically correct Hölderlin. Yet nor do we assume the right to string together "pieces" and "passages" from Hölderlin's poetry with whose aid we might, for instance, validate and illuminate the current age and thus make Hölderlin "relevant to today." The "historiographically factual" and "correct" Hölderlin and the Hölderlin "relevant to today" are both equally objectionable "products" of a manner of proceeding that from the outset simply does not want to hear *what* the poet says. Instead, one takes present-day historiographical consciousness and present-day "lived experience" to be "what is true" in itself and subjects the poet and his word to this standard, which is supposed to be true simply because it is current.

§2. The attempt to think the word poetized by Hölderlin

The one and only thing that the lecture course attempts is solely to think what Hölderlin has poetized, and in thinking it, to come to know it. That which has been poetized in this poetry, however, resides in something that already *is*, yet that we in fact never and nowhere encounter so long as we inquire only within our commonplace reality for something correspondingly real.

If, however, we are venturing to think what is poetized in Hölderlin's word, are we not then subjecting the poetizing to the torture rack of concepts? "Poems," after all, have to be "experienced," and to "lived experience" there belongs in the first instance "feeling," or in zoological terms, "instinct." We do not propose to disturb anyone here in his or her "lived experience." But we are going to give "thinking" a try.

Perhaps "thinking" is more closely related to "poetizing" than is our much-vaunted "lived experience." Admittedly, we remain in the dark concerning the essence of the inner relation between poetizing and thinking. This is why our enterprise is immediately in danger of being misconstrued. The attempt to think the word poetized by Hölderlin appears to diminish Hölderlin's poetry in another respect. In this case, by reducing it, not to a repository for timely "quotes," but to an archaeological site from which building blocks are amassed for a self-constructed "system of philosophy." This latter type of plundering of the poetic work may well be still worse than the former. Yet if our concern is with thinking, that by no means signifies that we are intent upon something like a "system of philosophy" or concerned with "philosophy" at all. Here it is a matter neither of "philosophy" nor of "poesy."

The sole thing that matters is the attempt to think what is poetized in Hölderlin's poetry, to think that which is poetized itself and this alone. We are not concerned with Hölderlin, or with Hölderlin's "work" in the sense of an achievement of this poet, or even with Hölderlin's work as an "example" of the universal essence of poetry and art. It is solely a matter of that which this work sets to work, and that always means what it conceals and keeps sheltered within itself. Our singular concern is whether that which is called upon and called forth in the poetizing word takes up a relation to us of its own accord and accordingly speaks to us; whether this claim, if it speaks, concerns our essence, and not, for instance, only the "subjective" "lived experience" of a few individuals among us or the "lived experience" of "communities" presently at hand. The issue is whether the essence of the planetary human being, who has become unhistorical, can be made to totter and thereby brought to reflect.

§3. That which is poetized in the word of essential poetizing "poetizes over and beyond" the poet and those who hear this word

In setting out to think what is poetized in Hölderlin's poetry, we are not thereby attempting to bring to our intuition what Hölderlin himself envisioned in the first saying of his poetry. This no research can ever discover and no thinking can ever come to discern. Even presupposing that such an impossibility were in fact possible, supposing therefore that we could transpose ourselves precisely back into the erstwhile sphere of Hölderlin's vision, this in no way guarantees that in so doing we would be thinking what Hölderlin's word poetizes. For the word of the true poet each time poetizes over and beyond the poet's own intention and vision.[1]

The poetizing word names something that comes over the poet and transposes him into a belonging that he has not created, one that he himself can only follow. What is named in the poetizing word never stands before the poet like a surveyable object. What is poetized not only takes the poet into a belonging transformative of his essence. What is poetized itself still shelters within it something closed off, something that surpasses the force of the word. *The word of the poet and that which is poetized in it poetize over and beyond the poet and his saying.* When we assert this about "poetry," we always mean only *essential* poetry. It alone poetizes what is inceptual; it alone releases what is original into its own arrival.

Like every activity in which human ability plays a part, poetizing too admittedly also has its derivative and aberrant forms. We should not scoff at these and regard them as altogether superfluous. It may very well happen that at a "poets' convention" three hundred writers get together, some good and some of lesser prominence, and that not a single poet is among them. This should not surprise us if we consider that it may perhaps take centuries for a single poet to emerge, and that when he does emerge, he may scarcely be recognized immediately even by those capable of judgment.

On our path we are seeking the word of an essential poetizing. The word of the poet is never his own nor his own property. The poet stands astonished and solitary within the mystery of the word, which is only seemingly his own, as does anyone who attempts to approach the realm that the word opens up and at the same time veils. Above all, the poetizing word poetizes over and beyond those who are to hear it.

In attempting to think that which is poetized in Hölderlin's poetry, we are not, then, pursuing the impossible task of reproducing and reenacting Hölderlin's erstwhile "inner world" or his frame of mind. In contrast to this, we must seek a path toward intimating that which poetizes over beyond the poet himself, and from this intimating unfold an essential *knowing* within whose ambit all our other bits of knowledge first take root and find a foothold.

§4. The essential singularity of Hölderlin's poetizing is not subject to any demand for proof

Yet is not this entire undertaking presumptuous, namely, to think in the direction of that which has poetized over and beyond even the poet? Why is it that latecomers should more readily know a path leading us to whatever came to the poet? From where should those who have not been called more readily have the ability to hold out in that realm from which even this poet himself was taken away into the protection of derangement? Above all, however, until now we have been forgetting this one thing, that with such an intention we are singling out Hölderlin's poetizing in an unusual way, without offering the slightest proof of the singularity that our thinking is thereby according him. For manifestly it cannot be some kind of "artistic taste" or an intangible "aesthetic" preference that here decides that we want to grant a hearing to the word of precisely this poet and not to the "work" of another poet. How can we prove that Hölderlin's word poetizes something inceptual?

A sober reconsideration of our intent shows how we are everywhere lining up one audacious claim after another. At most, everything remains only the personal view of a particular individual. It looks as though we are arbitrarily privileging only this one poet from the gallery of poets historiographically arrayed (Klopstock, Lessing, Herder, Goethe, Schiller, Kleist). Perhaps because Hölderlin is now "in fashion," as it has been said. In accordance with its essence, fashion tends to be eager for novelty and change and limited duration. For us, however, Hölderlin was already "in fashion" before the First World War. Unlike many who carried an edition of Goethe's *Faust*, quite a few carried Hölderlin's poems with them in their packs. This fashion has thus already extended over three decades—a remarkable fashion—which is to say that "fashion" is not in play here. Yet neither is our giving preference to this one poet over others on the basis of some kind of historiographical reckoning.

Nonetheless, the appearance initially persists that our intention arises only from the contingent opinion of someone who ventures one such an attempt to provide a pointer to Hölderlin's word. What this pointer is able to offer lacks all binding force, therefore, when considered and assessed on its own terms. Such binding force, if it arises, can indeed come only from the poetizing word of Hölderlin's poetry itself.

We can thus attempt to set out on the path to Hölderlin's word only with the prospect of going astray. However—it is not just this pointer that remains presumptuous. What remains presumptuous is also the demand for "proofs" that are first meant to assure us beforehand by way of "explanations" that a word is saying something essential here. It indeed appears to be a sign of a well-considered and sober approach when before all else we demand proof that it is an essential poetizing that is speaking here. Yet the demand for advance proofs of what Hölderlin's word is capable of poetizing is, in truth, a denigration of this word; it is, in truth, the elevation of our own ego to the authoritative tribunal before which this word must first prove itself. Despite a perhaps established "aesthetic" appreciation of its "beauty," this demand for advance proofs of the essentiality of this poetizing is fundamentally a resistance to the claim of this word. For all its eagerness to become acquainted with it, such a way of approaching the word of this poetizing would seek to place nothing at stake. Thus an indeterminacy lies at the beginning of our path to Hölderlin's word, because there is no one among us who brings with him proof attesting to the fact that he is the one called upon to be the interpreter.

For this reason, the pointer that we attempt to provide here serves only as an initial encouragement to venture a path to the word of this poet; "a" path, but not "the" path. No one is entitled to think that he or she knows "the" path. Even the particular path that we are trying here must often remain a detour.

§5. The poetizing word and language as means of communication. Planetary alienation in relation to the word

The following pointer to some of Hölderlin's poetizing says certain things that, according to the letter of the word, cannot be found within the "poems," even things that cannot be claimed to be poetized in the "poems." Nonetheless, these pointers may assist in making the poetizing word more audible.

It remains proper to the poetizing word that it oscillates within a peculiarly gathered multiplicity of meaning. We say "remains," for the poetizing word remains most closely faithful to the essence of the word, insofar as every genuine word poetizes. Admittedly, in order to see this, we may not adhere to the conception of language that has long since been provided to us. According to that conception, language is an instrument for reaching agreement, which, in keeping with the increase in traffic, becomes a vehicle for communication and must bring itself into line with this aspect. Such a vehicle demands a use of words that is unambiguous and concise. For example, one no longer says Auswärtige Amt [Foreign Affairs Office], but instead the abbreviation "AA," and those who speak this way imagine themselves to be especially initiated. However, this modern and American phonetic construction "AA" is already ambiguous. It can also mean Aufklärungs-Abteilung [Instructional Division]; thus, an administrator who is otherwise a professor of German literary history recently informed me that he is busy with the creation of new "AAs."

One now speaks and writes of the "uni" and means the university. The hideousness of this linguistic construction perhaps corresponds to the degree of understanding one is able to summon for the aforementioned institution.

This Americanization of language and increasing erosion of language to a technical instrument or vehicle of communication does not stem from some casual neglect or superficiality on the part of individuals or entire professions and organizations. This process has metaphysical grounds and for this very reason cannot be "stopped,"[2] which would indeed also only be a technical intervention.

We must reflect upon the event that is transpiring [sich ereignet] in this process: that the contemporary planetary human being no longer has "time" left for the word (that is, for the highest distinction of his essence). All of this has nothing to do with the corruption or purification of language. This process—in which the word is denied time and a phonetic abbreviation is seized upon—extends back into grounds upon which Western history, and thereby European, and thereby modern planetary "history" in general, rests.

To this alienation in relation to the word there corresponds the process through which "poetizing" is transformed into a "politico-cultural" "instrument," a process whose course displays the same uniformity in Europe, America, East Asia, and Russia. We fail to understand this process when, in response to it, we arrogantly assign it the label "cultural decline."

For us, this planetary alienation in relation to the word is just one of those manifestations that exposes the path leading to the word to peculiar obstacles and misinterpretations.

1. "Thinking" that which is poetized

This lecture course attempts to provide a pointer to a few of Hölderlin's poems. Those that have been selected are: "Remembrance," "The Ister," "The Titans," "Mnemosyne," and "Ripe, bathed in fire . . ." For now, we offer no grounds for this selection. Only the inner connection of these poems themselves can make visible the unity that provides a legitimate ground for this selection. Yet only when each one of these poems speaks purely in itself does their connection also come to the fore—that which we superficially enough name a "connection," yet which in truth is indeed a "unity" of a unique kind.

At the risk of at first still floundering in the indeterminate, we initially said what the lecture course does not intend. The lecture course does not claim to make a contribution to research into the "life and works" of Hölderlin. The lecture course does not at all intend to be historiographical, that is, to explore something from the past by referring it back to something else in the past and explaining it in such terms, an explanation whereby what is past is supposedly clarified and presented as what is correct. The lecture course, therefore, does not aim at the historiographically "correct" Hölderlin either.

Yet just as little is the lecture course concerned with constructing from corresponding quotations a Hölderlin "relevant to the present." All created works that are ever compelled to become public in some form or other must also put up with being used arbitrarily for altogether alien purposes. Yet here, too, for example, a poem by Hölderlin can bring comfort and consolation to some through earnest engagement. By the same token, however, many are able to discover in Hölderlin's hymns only an inflated fervor from which they turn away, since such fare is not fitting for a strong race of people. The lecture course does not intend to engage in such "dealing" with Hölderlin's poetry, which fluctuates from year to year and is often tossed back and forth in crude oppositions, while all the time attempting to remain relevant to the present. What, then, does it intend?

The lecture course attempts to think that which is poetized in Hölderlin's hymns. Thinking that which is poetized? Would that not mean transforming Hölderlin's poetry into philosophy or placing it in the service of a particular philosophy? No. To think what is poetized here means to attain a kind of knowing from which we let what is poetized in this poetry be what it, of itself, is and first will be. For us, who are not poets, that which is poetized can be poetic only through our thinking the poetizing word. What "thinking" means here can come to light for us only in carrying it through. The task is to think that which is poetized in Hölderlin's hymnal poetry.

Yet the poetizing word poetizes over and beyond both itself and the poet—the poetizing word opens up and encloses an abundance of wealth that is inexhaustible because it is inceptual, and that is to say, it belongs to what is simple. If one therefore wanted to attempt to make accessible the poetizing word by endeavoring to trace the inner world of Hölderlin's erstwhile "lived experience," transposing oneself back into his state of mind, then that would be to remain in a multiple sense wholly outside the domain that the word opens up in its poetizing. That which is poetized is in no way that which Hölderlin for his part intended in the representation of his inner world but is rather that which intended him when it called him into this vocation of being a poet. Strictly speaking, the poet is himself in the first instance poetized by that which he has to poetize.

Yet where now are rod and staff to be found, with whose aid we might venture into this domain of that which is poetized? Indeed, what we are seeking borders on the impossible. Everything here can miscarry. Every pointer remains a conjecture. Nowhere do we encounter anything binding. Above all, there are no authorities here to whose pronouncements we might submit, just because they presumed to stand over the word of poetizing. Only the latter, however, can alone and on its terms be the word and therefore "have the word."

2. Hearing that which is poetized is hearkening: waiting for the coming of the inceptual word

If, however, we consider that the word is something said, then we are not left wandering entirely in a void. Yet how should we hear it? What is it that is poetizing in the word? Must we not, after all, venture something for our part, something that concerns the essence of poetizing and determines it in advance? Hearing is, to be sure, not just a receiving of the word. Hearing is first and foremost a hearkening. Hearkening entails putting on hold all other modes of apprehending. To hearken is to be completely alone with that which is coming. Hearkening is being gathered in the direction of a singular and readied reaching out into the domain of an arrival, a domain in which we are not yet at home. Hearers must first be hearkeners, and hearkeners are those who venture and wait at the same time. We have already ventured something when we said that the poetizing word poetizes over beyond itself and the poet. This is for the time being an assertion. It entails the acknowledgment that something inceptual comes to pass [*sich ereignet*] in the word.

We have ventured something. Are we also those who wait? We have to be if we want to hear the word of the poetizing. For only the poetizing itself can make known to us whether and to what extent it is of such an essence as the assertion claims. In this, both the essence of the word and of language in general must come to light for us. Yet here, too, we, for our part, can in turn contribute a few things, if right at the beginning we attend more precisely to a routine phenomenon of "language" and of the word, namely, the "polysemy" of every word.

Most of the time we regard such multiplicity of meaning as a deficiency, since it readily gives rise to misunderstandings and becomes a means whereby we are led astray. For this reason, we endeavor to eliminate the deficiency that resides within such multiplicity of meaning. What is demanded is lack of ambiguity in discourse and accuracy of the word. When language is made into a vehicle of communication it has to conform to being a means of transportation and conform to traffic regulation. In order to save time and increase the force of its impact, the word is abbreviated and appears as a compressed amalgam of letters. The word becomes a traffic sign like the arrow, the circle with a line through it, or the triangle.

Yet for a long time now, namely, since the very emergence of metaphysics in Plato's thinking, there has existed a special academic discipline in which one can supposedly learn, among other things, the production of univocal word-meanings and "concepts." This discipline is still today called "Logic."

§6. The univocity of "logic" and the wealth of the genuine word out of the inexhaustibility of the commencement

That "Logic" demands univocity from word-meanings, and that likewise the practical, technical, and scientific use of language as a means of transportation drives in quite different ways toward what is unambiguous—all this attests only to how decisively the word and its telling, taken on its own terms, *is* multiple in meaning. This multiplicity of meaning, and what we name as such, does not originarily rest upon a negligence in the use of words but is rather the already-misconstrued reflection of the word's essential wealth. As soon as we regard language in terms of "univocity" and "polysemy," we are already conceiving the word according to the standards of "Logic."

In truth, however, every genuine word has its concealed and manifold spaces in which it resonates. Essential poetizing attests to itself, first, in that that which it has poetized maintains itself solely within the realm of these spaces resonating over beyond themselves, and in its speaking from out of such spaces. The wealth belonging to every genuine word—which is emphatically never a mere jumble of scattered meanings but rather the simple unity of what is essential—has its ground in the fact that it names something inceptual, and every commencement is at once inexhaustible and singular. For this reason, too, a singular kind of determinacy is proper to poetizing. Because it includes this wealth of meaning, poetizing demands from thinking a higher kind of lawfulness and rigor. The thinking of a concept of mathematics or physics, by contrast, is bound solely to the univocity of the exact. The exact can be determined in its own way only because it is found "wanting," and this want finds its support in the quantitative. By contrast, the carefulness of that thinking which enters into the poetizing word cannot let itself be satisfied with "definitions," yet nor can it lose itself in the indeterminacy of vague and haphazard opinion. The wealth of the poetizing word, which resides in the determinacy of that which is poetized, can therefore only be attained, if at all, upon paths that are fundamentally different from the usual understanding of statements and propositions belonging to linguistic communication and presentation.

It may initially appear as sheer caprice when we conceive of the path to that which is poetized in Hölderlin's poetry as a thinking. Assuming, however, that this path is an appropriate one, then our choice of this path presupposes that Hölderlin's poetizing is in itself a thinking. If this is the case, then we must before all else endeavor to participate in the accomplishment of this type of thinking. This thinking, however, can become manifest only in the poetizing itself, whether through this thinking being accomplished in an unspoken manner in the poetizing and having entered into the poetizing word, or through the fact that the poetizing itself in addition tells specifically "of" such thinking [*Denken*]. The latter is in fact the case. Within the sphere of Hölderlin's hymns there stands a poem that is titled "Remembrance" ["*Andenken*"].

§7. Remark on the editions of Hölderlin's works

The texts that form the basis for this lecture course are taken from the edition whose decisive volumes (I, IV, and V) were compiled by Norbert von Hellingrath, who died in battle in 1916 as a twenty-eight-year-old at

Verdun. Hölderlin's hymns can be found in volume IV of von Hellingrath's edition.[2]

The Zinkernagel edition (published by Inselverlag) can also be used.[3] The poems elucidated in the lecture course are to be found in volumes I and V of that edition.

A very fine and meticulous special edition of the hymns was published several years ago in 1938 by Klostermann in Frankfurt am Main (now out of print).[4]

Without the repeated attempt to draw near to the word of the poet, your attending this lecture course will lack the requisite foothold.

---

2 Hölderlin, *Sämtliche Werke*, Historical-Critical Edition, begun by Norbert von Hellingrath, continued by Friedrich Seebass and Ludwig von Pigenot (Berlin, 1923), volume III (1922); volumes I, II, IV, V, VI (second edition, 1923). Roman numerals designate the volume, Arabic designate the page number.

3 Hölderlin, *Sämtliche Werke und Briefe in fünf Bänden*, Critical-Historical Edition by Franz Zinkernagel (Leipzig), volume I (1922); volume II (1914); volume III (1915); volume IV (1921); volume V (1926).

4 Friedrich Hölderlin, *Hymnen*, ed. Eduard Lachmann (Frankfurt am Main, 1938); second edition (1943).

Main Part

"Remembrance"

This poem was first published in Seckendorf's "Musenalmanach for 1808" (cf. IV, 61ff.). It was probably composed around 1803–1804; only the last strophe is preserved in its handwritten form.

ANDENKEN

Der Nordost wehet,
Der liebste unter den Winden
Mir, weil er feurigen Geist
Und gute Fahrt verheißet den Schiffern.
Geh aber nun und grüße
Die schöne Garonne,
Und die Gärten von Bourdeaux
Dort, wo am scharfen Ufer
Hingehet der Steg und in den Strom
Tief fällt der Bach, darüber aber
Hinschauet ein edel Paar
Von Eichen und Silberpappeln;

Noch denket das mir wohl und wie
Die breiten Gipfel neiget
Der Ulmwald, über die Mühl',
Im Hofe aber wächset ein Feigenbaum.
An Feiertagen gehn
Die braunen Frauen daselbst
Auf seidnen Boden,
Zur Märzenzeit,
Wenn gleich ist Nacht und Tag,
Und über langsamen Stegen,
Von goldenen Träumen schwer,
Einwiegende Lüfte ziehen.

Es reiche aber,
Des dunkeln Lichtes voll,
Mir einer den duftenden Becher,
Damit ich ruhen möge; denn süß

Wär' unter Schatten der Schlummer.
Nicht ist es gut
Seellos von sterblichen
Gedanken zu seyn. Doch gut
Ist ein Gespräch und zu sagen
Des Herzens Meinung, zu hören viel
Von Tagen der Lieb',
Und Thaten, welche geschehen.

Wo aber sind die Freunde? Bellarmin
Mit dem Gefährten? Mancher
Trägt Scheue, an die Quelle zu gehn;
Es beginnet nemlich der Reichtum
Im Meere. Sie,
Wie Maler, bringen zusammen
Das Schöne der Erd' und verschmähn
Den geflügelten Krieg nicht, und
Zu wohnen einsam, jahrlang, unter
Dem entlaubten Mast, wo nicht die Nacht durchglänzen
Die Feiertage der Stadt,
Und Saitenspiel und eingeborener Tanz nicht.

Nun aber sind zu Indiern
Die Männer gegangen,
Dort an der luftigen Spiz'
An Traubenbergen, wo herab
Die Dordogne kommt
Und zusammen mit der prächt'gen
Garonne meerbreit
Ausgehet der Strom. Es nehmet aber
Und giebt Gedächtniß die See,
Und die Lieb' auch heftet fleißige Augen.
Was bleibet aber, stiften die Dichter.

REMEMBRANCE

The northeasterly blows,
Most beloved of the winds
To me, for it promises fiery spirit
And good voyage to mariners.
But go now and greet
The beautiful Garonne,

And the gardens of Bordeaux
There, by the steep bank
Where the footbridge crosses and into the river
Deep falls the brook, yet over it
Keep watch a noble pair
Of oaks and silver poplars;

Still it thinks its way to me, and how
The spread of tree tops, the elm forest
Bows over the mill,
But in the courtyard grows a fig tree.
On holidays go
The brown women thereat
On silken ground,
In March time,
When night and day are equal,
And over slow footbridges,
Heavy with golden dreams,
Lulling breezes draw.

Yet may someone reach me,
Full of dark light,
The fragrant cup,
That I may rest; for sweet
Would be the slumber among shadows.
It is not good
To be soulless of mortal
Thoughts. Yet good
Is a dialogue and to say
The heart's opinion, to hear much
Of days of love,
And deeds that occur.

Yet where are the friends? Bellarmine
And companion? Many a one
Is shy of going to the source;
For wealth indeed begins
In the ocean. They,
Like painters, bring together
The beautiful of the Earth and do not spurn
The winged war, and
To dwell in solitude, year long, beneath

The defoliate mast, where there gleam not through the night
The holidays of the town,
Nor the music of strings nor native dance.

But now to Indians
The men have gone,
There on the breezy headland
On vineyard slopes, where down
Comes the Dordogne
And together with the magnificent
Garonne the river
Spreads into the ocean. Yet what takes
And gives memory is the sea,
And love, too, fixes with intensity our eyes.
Yet what remains, the poets found.

§8. A word of warning about merely admiring the beauty of the poem

We might initially simply marvel and almost be overcome with admiration, for the wonder and the "beauty" of this poem are manifest. If, however, we were simply to persist in such an attunement, then despite our apparently being affected by the poem, we would in fact remain untouched by it. We would treat the poem only as an object that the creative effort of a poet has accomplished. We would be admiring a success; we would be lingering over one occurrence within the history of poetic achievements. We would be marveling at something we possess, taking joy in a "cultural" treasure.

We fall into error in believing that the very assessment that a German poem formerly achieved such "greatness" is itself what is great already. And it may remain an open question what it really means when we call something "great." The secret of what is often called "great" in this manner indeed lies in the fact that it cannot be measured, which is precisely why the designation "great" is inappropriate. Moreover, this designation thinks what it thus names not *in terms of what is itself great* or in terms of what it is, and which can as a consequence first be called great by us. In referring to something great or even something "really great," we always mean this—if we mean anything at all—from the perspective of what is small. Something deceptive is at work here, something connected with the extravagance of historiographical representation. One believes that simply in proclaiming something to be great, one already has a part in greatness oneself and is great.

Marveling at the "beauty" of this poem can be genuine. Nonetheless, despite all our admiration for the poem, we remain outside of the domain of the poetizing word. In this way, what is poetized in this poetizing does not touch our essence. Our reception of the poem, however imbued with feeling and obsessed with taste it may be, together with our pronouncements concerning such "lived experiencing," remain stuck in the realm of enjoyment. We merely circle around our own states of mind and deny our essence to that which is poetized itself.

But what is that?

§9. Establishing a preliminary understanding about "content" and what is poetized in the poem

That which is poetized is surely that which is said in the word. What is contained in the word we call the "content." We can grasp this by "specifying the contents." Even if the poem did have a "content" that could be specified and reproduced like the "content" of a scientific treatise or a "factual report," we would then still need to ask whether this content of the poem coincides with what this poetizing poetizes. Does our "specifying the contents" already grant us a relation to what is poetized in the poem? We leave this question open. However, we must also concede that we cannot pass over all that is clearly talked about in the poem, above all, therefore, whatever belongs to the realm of what is factual and evident.

The poem names Bordeaux, the Garonne, and the Dordogne; it describes the people and places of southern France. We even know that Hölderlin traveled through Strasbourg and Lyon on his way to Bordeaux in the last days of 1801 in order to take up the position of house tutor there. Before his departure, he writes the following to his friend Böhlendorff on December 4, 1801 (V, 321f.):

> And now, farewell, my dear friend, until you hear more from me. I am now full of parting. I have not wept in so long. Yet it has cost me bitter tears, resolving now to leave my fatherland, perhaps forever. For what do I have more precious in the world? But they have no use for me. I wish to, and indeed must, remain German, even if the exigencies of the heart and of nourishment should drive me to Tahiti.

The word pronounced here—"But they have no use for me"—would also apply to his stay in Bordeaux. Already at the beginning of May 1802, Hölderlin returned to Germany, presumably via Paris, and arrived back at his mother's in Nürtingen in the second week of June. "But they have no use for me."

Toward the end of this year, on December 2, 1802, Hölderlin once again writes to Böhlendorff (V, 327): "My dear friend! I have not written you for a long time, have been in France in the meantime and seen the sad, solitary Earth; I have seen the cottages of Southern France and individual beauties, men and women, who grew up amid the anxiety of patriotic doubt and hunger. The powerful element, the fire of the heavens and the reticence of the people, their life in nature, and their restrictedness and contentment, continually captivated me, and as one says of heroes, I can indeed say that Apollo has struck me."

The two letters to Böhlendorff cited here grant us the richest insights into the poet's still barely illuminated thinking around this decisive time. Initially, we have cited only those passages from them that attest to Hölderlin's sojourn in southern France. In keeping with this, the poem we have just read is clearly a recollection of his sojourn in France. It reports on the basis of a "recollection" of a past "lived experience" and is therefore fittingly given the title "Remembrance." Norbert von Hellingrath is of the opinion that, "in contrast to the hymns," this poem has "the personal lived experiences of Hölderlin the *man* (not the poet) as its object" (IV, 300). Although it "approaches the poetic style of the hymns," von Hellingrath includes this poem among Hölderlin's "lyric" poems in the establishment of Hölderlin's works in his seminal edition.

Still, we must ask whether this poem "Remembrance" merely recollects personal lived experiences, whether it refers to anything like personal lived experiences, whether "Remembrance" here simply means the equivalent of a recollection of something past. Perhaps the poem is neither "lyrical" nor "hymnal." Perhaps we must set aside all such labels, so that they do not lead our view and our inner ear astray in advance. For we immediately catch ourselves talking "about" the poem once more, instead of letting its word speak to us.

Certainly the poem names Bordeaux; it "gives an account," as it were, of the landscape there, of the sea and of the people there. Yet even if we just "take it in" quite superficially, we also encounter a question in the poem. The fourth strophe begins: "Yet where are the friends?" And in the third strophe we are told: "Yet good / Is a dialogue . . ." The concluding strophe says of the sea that it gives and takes "memory." Passages and moments of pure lucidity and simple delight alternate with passages and moments of complete obscurity and hidden terror. In order to indicate, if only superficially, the rich oscillation and expansive character found in this poetizing, we may note that the poem entitled "Remembrance" concludes with the following line:

Was bleibet aber, stiften die Dichter.

Yet what remains, the poets found.

Here there is talk of founding, of the grounding of something to come, not of the memory of something past. We are told of that which remains, not of that which passes and is past. If we now already ponder the fact that it is only at the end of Hölderlin's poems that everything is gathered together, and that their authentic meaning quite often first comes to the fore in an unmediated way, then the relations between the poem's end and its title—which after all is supposed to indicate the whole—become thoroughly enigmatic.

In addition to all of this, and prior to all the things that could be cited here concerning the "content" of the poem, there presumably lies a cohesion that initially remains concealed. Even the internal coherence of the five strophes is obscure. The beginning and end of the poem are opaque in their relation to one another. One does not first need to forcibly "search for mysteries" in this poem in order to be instructed about the fact that it is not "readily understandable." It is not understandable, provided that we listen to the whole poem as a unity rather than delighting in individual "images" and relegating the remainder to some vague attunement. Why is the poem obscure? Because we do not know what is poetized in it, nor are we at first acquainted with any path leading to it. For this reason, we should not shun detours. For this reason, we must slowly lose the habit of looking for a "content" and being satisfied with specifying it.

This one, unifying thing, to which the poem presumably owes its hidden cohesion, we at first know of only in the form of the opaque relations between the strophes and lines. That which carries and determines the poem can be only that which is poetized. To be sure, one might indeed be inclined to the opposite opinion, namely, that what is poetized is surely tied to the poem as this linguistic construct that lies before us and is carried by the latter. Yet in that case we would once again be equating what is poetized with the content of the poem. We have already called into question this very move.

REVIEW

1. The wealth of the poetizing word

We are seeking that which is poetized in the word of Hölderlin's hymnal poetizing. We say, by way of assertion: the poetizing word poetizes over and beyond itself and the poet. And we note: the poetizing word fulfills, moreover, the original essence of the word, because each genuine word, as word, already poetizes. The poetizing word preserves its own kind of wealth and lawfulness that we grasp only poorly, or not at all, if we label it as mere polysemy; for in this way we measure such wealth in terms of the univocity of linguistic usage. All practical discourse of a technical, juridical, or moral kind, and every scientific statement, in its own way demands such univocity.

However, the wealth of the poetizing word does not conflict with its simplicity. It is only ever the fulfillment of such simplicity. That which is simple admittedly takes manifold forms. One variation of the simple is that which is paltry or sparse. Yet what is paltry is not worthless; to the contrary, it is that which is authentically useful and can be used, whereas what is simple in the sense of the poetic is useless. The wealth of the poetic word, which has its own configuration, cannot be reduced to "definitions."

Yet when we think the poetizing word and enter into its magic, we are not thereby thinking "inexactly"; for one can think inexactly only within a domain of the exact, insofar as it is there that one may find the lawfulness of the exact missing. Thinking the poetizing word stands entirely outside of the opposition between "exact" and "inexact," and yet still has its own rigor; but it is also for this reason always surrounded by the danger of missing this rigor. Such missing has its own consequences. One of its peculiarities is that those who fall victim to such misconstruals of the essential word mostly fail to "notice" these misconstruals and their consequences their entire lives. By contrast, mistakes in the construction of machinery show up right away and with urgency. When the interpretation of Hölderlin's poems goes astray with regard to what is authentic, this does not result in any damage in the same way as does the failure of a diesel engine, for instance, or the collapse of a bridge and the breech of a dam. If the interpretation of a thinker from the commencement of Western thinking thinks awry, then this is, as we say, "no big deal." The "world" still runs its course.

2. Poetizing and thinking as historical action

Yet one "day," on a day of our history, namely, something will indeed come to pass [sich ereignen] that is only the consequence of that inconspicuous going astray and that unnoticed thinking awry. Even then no one will take heed of this event [Ereignis] so long as poetizing and thinking are regarded only as matters of "culture," and "culture" is regarded as the business of relaxation and edification, matters for which the "Americans" have for decades been the "model." Western history resides in such a concealed undercurrent of undisclosed events that the Germans could one day resolve to finally leave the culture industry to that other "hemisphere."

A unique space opens up here of a historical action that does not require "deeds" in order to be effective and does not require "effects" in order to *be*.

This action is poetizing and thinking. And participating in such action has a corresponding inconspicuousness within a space that we all too readily assume is not there, because *we* are not familiar with it, since we evaluate everything only according to "success" and "degree." If these sought-after things remain absent, then the world immediately appears empty, and we ourselves no longer know what to do with ourselves. Yet this emptiness makes itself known only because we have sought fullness in the wrong place, and have failed to recognize the space of authentic wealth that is granted us. Certainly, this space of such responsibility can never be reached by giving speeches about it. Yet a hint in that direction is necessary here.

It is for this reason that we are, so to speak, attempting to "learn" the thinking of that which is poetized by "listening" to Hölderlin's poem "Remembrance." The poetizing of the poetry to which it belongs stems from an assuredness that announces itself in the word: "To find something great is much, yet much is still left . . ." ("Menon's Lament for Diotima," IV, 87, line 117).

3. The transformation of the biographical in that which is poetized

At first glance, the poem "Remembrance" appears only to bring Hölderlin's "personal lived experiences" into the tones of a song. This "lyrical" impression is amplified still further when we seek to draw information from the two letters written to his friend Böhlendorff, the first shortly before his trip to southern France, the second some time after his return. The latter even contains anticipatory resonances and linguistic echoes of the poem "Remembrance." We can use these letters as biographical and historiographical documents. There is no prohibition against doing so. Yet by doing so we run the risk of turning not only the poem into something biographical, but the two letters as well. We can, to be sure, exploit these letters as a repository of biographical curiosities, but we must then also admit that their fundamental trait remains concealed from us. For through these letters the poet speaks from out of a domain for which the biographical remains an occasion and opportunity, but only if it is integrated into the transformation accomplished by what is said. Of what use to us are biography, psychology, and historiography when we read in the letter from December 2, 1802 (V, 328):

> After a number of disruptions and turmoils in my soul, it was necessary for me to settle down for some time, and in the meantime I have been living in my paternal hometown.
> The more I study the nature of my homeland, the more powerfully it seizes me. The thunderstorm, not only in its highest manifestation,

but precisely in this regard, as a force and shape among the other forms of the heavens, forming the light in its effects, nationally and as a principle and mode of destiny, of something being holy to us, its course in coming and going, the characteristic element of the woods and the coming together of various aspects of nature in one region, that all holy locales of the Earth are gathered together around one locale, and the philosophical light around my window—this is now my delight; that I might remember how I have come all this way, to here!

What else can we say, other than that perhaps even the "biographical" notes that we can hunt down in the letter speak a different language than simple reports recounting past "lived experiences"?

Admittedly, even the poem "Remembrance" in its first, second, and fifth strophes initially sounds like a mere thinking back to something that has vanished. The simple act of making present the "images" depicted here could lead us to seek the proper "content" of the poem in the way these images are shaped. Yet how, from this approach, are we to understand the transition from the second into the third strophe, or the fact that at the beginning of the fourth strophe a question is posed, and that at the end of the entire poem a word concerning "the poets" is found? Each of these things on their own, but also with respect to their interconnection, remain enigmatic and obscure. Does that which is poetized consist of images to which "thoughts" are attached, or does that which is poetized reside in thoughts that are embellished by images? Or are neither of these two suppositions valid, because the very distinction between "images" and "thoughts" does not hit the mark and can never be sufficient to "hit upon" the essential unity of the poem?

We must seek a path toward the unity proper to that which is poetized. In so doing, we should not shy away from detours.

§10. That which is poetized in the poetizing and the "content" of the poem are not the same

We go so far as to assert: That which is poetized in the poetizing is not its "content," as though that which is poetized were like the water and the poetizing like the glass that it fills. That which is poetized is also not the "fruit" of the poetizing, as though that which is poetized were the apple and the poetizing the branch growing from the emergent tree. We can find absolutely no analogy for this relation. Yet this relation cannot be completely concealed and foreign to us either, if the word and language indeed belong to the essence of the human being. It may well be, on the other hand, that the relations of the word to the human being, and of the human essence to the word, have been disrupted. It could very well be that we know all kinds of things about poetic works in a historiographical manner, that all this knowledge has already become unsurveyable for us, and that, despite this, we are nevertheless not in a position—indeed for this very reason no longer in a position—to hear the poetizing word of this poetizing.

The assertion that what may perhaps be cited as the content of what has been poetized is not, as yet, what has been poetized in the poetizing should not in any way be taken to mean that listening to what the word of the poem indeed immediately says is something we could dispense with, as though we possessed a magic charm that could relieve us of the burden of carefully heeding the word in its immediacy. Our assertion that the content of the poem and that which is poetized in the poetizing are not the same thing implies only this: we may not allow that which we apprehended in our first hearing of the word to coagulate into a "content," nor to regard this coagulum as the truth of the poetizing. We must, therefore, above all listen to the word in its immediacy, and perhaps with greater care than can be accomplished by tracking down a content. To this end, it is first of all necessary to attentively follow the unfolding of the five strophes, even at the risk that the illusion continues to persist that we thereby arrive at nothing other than a "specification of contents." The "poem" initially still lies before us as a written and spoken construction from which we derive something; we do not yet stand *within* that realm which it, as word, is.

Part One

Entry into the Realm of the Poem as Word

§11. The beginning and conclusion of the poem

> Der Nordost wehet,
> Der liebste unter den Winden
> Mir, weil er feurigen Geist
> Und gute Fahrt verheißet den Schiffern.

> The northeasterly blows,
> Most beloved of the winds
> To me, for it promises fiery spirit
> And good voyage to mariners.

"The northeasterly"—that wind is named which, in the broad regions of the Swabian homeland, sweeps and clears the sky with its biting coolness, clearing a space for the fire from the heavens, "the sun," a space in which its illumination and glow can unfold. This wind clears the air. In such an air, that which is cold, bold, and unerring opens up; this air directs us into the open distances, yet in such a way that it makes our vision steadfast and capable of seeing all things loom forth and repose, as their outline emerges from all haze and mist. This wind brings an assured transparency into the world, grants a pervasive constancy to the weather, and anchors our attunement. A later draft that may even be related to "Remembrance" also names the "northeasterly"; in this draft it is said of the migratory birds, of the "starlings" (IV, 257):

> Und ihnen machet waker
> Scharfwehend die Augen der Nordost . . .

> And their eyes are made steadfast
> By the northeasterly's bite . . .

"Remembrance" begins with the word "The northeasterly blows." This sounds like the ascertainment of a fact, although we are not told directly when it blows. Nor is it immediately clear where it blows. "The north-easterly blows"—and not the southwesterly. Is the northeasterly blowing now, as the poet begins to compose this poem? Is the first line meant, perhaps, to ascertain the direction of the wind at the time when Hölderlin is beginning to write down this poem? Perhaps everything is the other way round instead. The poem names the northeasterly, not because there is a northeasterly air at the moment of the poetic composition of this poem. Rather, it is because this entire poem must be said from out of *that which* it poetizes that there lies already over everything the cool clarity and pure decidedness of a simple knowing. This is why it must begin with the nam-ing of the northeasterly.

"The northeasterly blows." This is neither the factual ascertaining of wind conditions, nor the description of a contingent weather situation, nor a "poetological" "framing" for subsequent "thoughts." "The northeasterly blows": with this first line there begins already the mystery. Indeed, this line contains the mystery of the entire poem. This first line resonates in every line that follows. As we transition from each strophe to the next, we must hear this line. This first line attains its full resonance only in the last line.

It might now appear as though we were looking for mysteries even in those places where "rational human beings" find none. And yet we must assert the following: "The northeasterly blows"—taken by itself, this word indeed leaves indeterminate the point in time and the location of that of which it speaks. Nevertheless, it names the time-space from out of which comes the attuning favor of the poetizing that is now needed and is yet to come, in order that this poetizing may fulfill its essence and that poets may be. "The northeasterly blows"—that is to say: the time-space of poetizing, of the poetizing that is also poetized in this poem, stands open. We avoid saying that the first line is an "image" for this "thought." We are indicating only that, if the first line says what we have named, then between the begin-ning of the poem and its conclusion there lies an essential relation that at once embraces this poem in its totality: "The northeasterly blows"—"Yet what remains, the poets found."

What stands between the first and last lines of this poem is drawn out discursively and in writing in the sequential ordering of its strophes. The sequence of lines is an accumulation of words, and yet we name what is said and what speaks as a whole "the word" of the poem—more pre-cisely, the poem as this word. Because our pointer concerning Hölderlin's poem moves within this realm of the word, already with the first line we must give thought to something essential concerning the word and language.

§12. *Concerning language: the poetizing word and sounding words*

"Language" is the faculty of the word. What gets formed in the process of speaking we call the "words" of a language. Words [*Wörter*], however, are something other than the word [*Worte*].[3] The statements of the thinker Heraclitus, for example, indeed consist of words, yet we do not say "the words" of Heraclitus, but the word [*die Worte*]. There are words only where there is language. Yet language itself exists only where there is the word.[4] The word is the origin of language. Yet what does this mean: "the word" as the origin of language? In the unfolding of this lecture course, we are to learn to give thought to some aspects of this question.

Language enunciates the word [*Worte*], and what is enunciated can disintegrate into "words." As a result of long habituation, we are all too inclined to determine the essence of language and of the word on the basis of such words, and thus also to interpret on this basis the relationship of the poem as a linguistic construction to what is poetized. We thus arrive at the view that that which is said, which is something poetized, is itself reproduced in the sequence of sounds and words of the poem.

And yet words [*Wörter*] are never reproductions or copies of that which they signify. Onomatopoeic words [*Worte*] like "cuckoo," "buzz," "whizz," or "hiss" appear to contradict this. Yet even the articulated sound "cuckoo" is a word only whenever we mean and say "the" cuckoo: what this "the" means, and what it conveys and imparts to the articulated sound "cuckoo"—none of this lies within the mere sounding of the reproduced call of the bird, no matter how often, or how loud, or how imitative this sound resonates. Nonetheless, sound and sounding do belong in a certain manner to the "word" [*"Wort"*]; indeed, the way in which the sounds, the vowels, and the consonants are conjoined also in one respect contributes to the form of what we tend to call "the beauty" of a "language."

Why do we mention such "things"? To indicate that the essence of the word [*des Wortes*] (of words [*der Wörter*] and of the word [*der Worte*]) is indeed familiar to us in certain aspects, yet in truth is altogether hidden from us. For this very reason we find it difficult to grasp the unity of the sounding words and the poetizing word, as we simultaneously let ourselves enter the sequence of lines and strophes and nevertheless maintain a relation to that which is poetized in the poetizing word.

When we say "and nevertheless," then this seems to confirm an opposition between the word-form of the poetizing and that which is poetized. We may be of the opinion that that which is poetized is a separate "spiritual meaning," and the verbal sound [*Wortlaut*] of the poem its contingent "sensuous *image*" ["Sinn*bild*"]. Ever since Plato, the entire Western view of art has stood under the force of this distinction between "suprasensuous" and "sensuous." The "sensuous image"—as symbol—has the task of bringing the two together and conjoining them. "Language" itself becomes forced into this schema too, such that the articulated sound of the word is conceived as the "body," and the meaning of the word, on the other hand, as the "soul" or "spirit" of language.

§13. Language in our historical moment

Our relation to language, to words and to the word, has for a long time been confused, indeterminate, and without grounding. Language is like some present at hand thing; why should it, too, not be exploited as an instrument of "organization" and as something human beings arm themselves with, and be secured as a means of power and as a form of domination? No one today can exclude himself from this process, which is "metaphysical" in nature and remains withdrawn from the predilection, negligence, and zeal of the individual.

For this process of the "instrumentalization" of language does not have to proceed in a purely negative manner. Within this same sphere, it can call forth a countermovement that strives for a new "instrumentation" of language in order to achieve for it the highest degree of "accuracy." This relationship to language, which is, for example, embodied by Ernst Jünger, still belongs entirely to that metaphysical space determined by Nietzsche's interpretation of being as will to power. Just like "film," language is a way of arming oneself, a way through which the "Gestalt of the Worker" comes to dominate the "world." The word as a weapon of the highest order and of the deepest concern is distinguished only in degree, and not according to its essence, from the word in its Americanized form, which, in piecing together the first letters of its syllables and component parts, turns both the Auswärtige Amt [Ministry of Foreign Affairs] and the Aufklärungs-Abteilung [Instructional Division] into the "AA."

This technical instrumentation of the essence of language itself plays a role in shaping our historical moment. In a metaphysical, historical moment that is *determined in this way* we must indeed be instructed about our relationship—or distorted relationship—to language and to the word. It may then become clear to us that it is only through patient effort that we arrive at the path whereby we may apprehend Hölderlin's poem as the poetizing of what has been poetized.

§14. Preliminary consideration of the unity of the poem

To our immediate, indeterminate hearing, the first line, "The northeasterly blows," names an isolated occurrence within "nature" that can be sensuously experienced. To our fleeting reflection, the last line, "Yet what remains, the poets found," names an essential law in the supreme realm of "spirit"—if, for the purpose of a preliminary understanding, we are permitted to speak of "nature" and "spirit" in such general terms. Yet at the same time it became evident that the first line is not a description of nature, but rather names the favor of the poetic and its time-space. Correspondingly, the concluding line perhaps does not simply give us a didactic "sententia" about the essence of poetry, but, in speaking of what remains, in fact names "nature," without thereby depicting something that can be experienced.

When in advance we retrace the poem from its beginning and from its end in the direction of its as yet concealed unity, our inner ear is already becoming more concentrated. Even that which at first only appears as a tranquil description, "The northeasterly blows," will in the future, from time to time, become fuller and have more to say.

"The northeasterly blows." This is an unconditioned event, which here stands immediately in the word, and consequently is. "The northeasterly blows." Its blowing is arrival, and is a going that points and carries off into something futural. Everything is replete with coming. The title "Remembrance" becomes less and less fitting:

> Der Nordost wehet,
> Der liebste unter den Winden
> Mir . . .

> The northeasterly blows,
> Most beloved of the winds
> To me . . .

The northeasterly is singled out before all other winds. "Most beloved . . . to me . . ." Here Hölderlin speaks of himself. Certainly. But is it the I who is speaking and who judges the different winds and weather conditions in relation to the personal state he finds himself in? Is Hölderlin here expressing his "sensitivity to nature" through a depiction of nature in which the thought of the wind also plays a role? "Most beloved . . . to me . . ." With this "me" Hölderlin indeed means himself. Yet the I who speaks of itself there is not Hölderlin the person. The basis of this predilection for the northeasterly is not to be found in the personal leanings, wants, or biographical relationships of the human being Hölderlin; for the grounds for this predilection for the northeasterly, which immediately follow in the next lines, can in no way be traced back to the personal taste and "mode of lived experience" of Hölderlin the human being, and not at all to the mental or physical state that an individual human being finds himself in. Rather, the northeasterly is the most beloved of the winds "to me":

> . . . weil er feurigen Geist
> Und gute Fahrt verheißet den Schiffern.

> . . . for it promises fiery spirit
> And good voyage to mariners.

The northeasterly is named, and is singled out as the most beloved, in view of its relation to "mariners." Who are the "mariners"? Men, in any case, for whom the northeasterly is a promise, which is to say: advance notice, assurance, bestowal. All this in a twofold way: The northeasterly points the direction to where the spirit is fiery, and at the same time it carries and brings those who set forth into a "good voyage."

REVIEW

We have now taken our first step over the threshold in our attempt to interpret Hölderlin's poetry. The threshold is the place of transition in stepping from one domain into another. The domain familiar to us is the poem as a thing present at hand, as it were: the written, read, spoken phonetic construction. This is what lies before us; it is we who have the poem at our disposal and can make of it what we will. There has lately been talk of the "handling of poetry."

The other domain is the poem as the word, which *we* do not have before us, but that instead, *proceeding from itself*, is to take us up into the space of its truth. The word is never something we can "handle"; instead, the word will either "affect" us or pass right over us.

Both these domains, that of the linguistic construction present at hand and that of the word, would however never be captured if we were to conceive the former as the exterior and the latter as the interior. For this distinction between "outside" and "inside" still falls within that first domain, insofar as one attributes to the linguistic construction a meaning that it bears "within" itself as its "content."

Yet we are seeking something different here, something that will in general presumably entail a transformation in the relation of the word to ourselves. It is questionable whether such a transformation may be ventured outside the domain of Hölderlin's word. For this word, as the word of his hymnal poetizing, is singular, in a sense that is itself singular in turn. This word is like a solitary mountain range that, rising from an exigency that has emerged, first opens another space of truth around itself. Nothing in this poetizing is embellishment, and there are no blank spaces. This word is not a statement "about" something to someone who might assume power over the word.

We ourselves can no longer gauge the fact that our relation to the "word" is completely disrupted, and has been for decades, through the rampant production of idle scribble, through groundless idle talk and through idle and indiscriminate reading. For this reason we should also not expect to regain this relation to the word at a stroke, for instance by bringing into play our so-called "direct lived experience" when encountering a poem by Hölderlin. Heartfelt sensitivity and artistic intuition are fine things. Yet the question remains whether such recourse to "lived experience," even when it is genuine, does not in fact still remain within our already disrupted relation to the word, and thus is capable neither of recognizing, nor of overcoming this disruption.

To now reach even just the perimeter of the sphere of Hölderlin's word, a different and higher-level exertion is required, one that must pass through the clarity of a particular knowing. Such exertion is, among other things, reflected in the laboriousness of our interpretation. You may very well run up against this laboriousness. Well and good. You may very well consider this all an intellectual violation of the "artistic," which after all, as one hears, remains reserved in the first place for the domain of "feeling" and of "taste." Well and good. Yet you may also one day want to check whether a light has not suddenly been turned on for you as a result of this conceptual laboriousness.

The interpretation depends upon this alone. The interpretation is not being given for its own sake. The goal of genuine interpretation consists solely in making itself superfluous. The more complete an interpretation is in its construction, the more decisively it dismantles and thus effaces itself by its end, so that only the word of the poet speaks. If, by contrast, we take only what *we* understand and what *we* "feel" as the measure of what the poet may have said and may have been allowed to say, then we lack the first condition for all hearing, and that is: the quiet passion for the unsaid:

> Der Nordost wehet,
> Der liebste unter den Winden

> Mir, weil er feurigen Geist
> Und gute Fahrt verheißet den Schiffern.

> The northeasterly blows,
> Most beloved of the winds
> To me, for it promises fiery spirit
> And good voyage to mariners.

The time-space of bold clarity has opened itself up, and the poet himself knows himself within this open realm. This open realm is a being directed into the remoteness and assurance of that which is coming. The northeasterly promises "fiery spirit."

§15. Poetizing and the explanation of nature in modernity. On the theory of "image" and "metaphor"

The "fiery" initially refers to the particular "fire" that we call the sun. The second poem we shall draw attention to, "The Ister," begins thus (IV, 220):

> Jezt komme, Feuer!
> Begierig sind wir
> Zu schauen den Tag, . . .

> Now come, fire!
> Eager are we
> To see the day, . . .

Yet the same thing applies to the fire and the sun as to the wind, the northeasterly, which, proceeding from our accustomed habit, we "at first" take to be things of nature. From this perspective, we are tempted to say that sun and wind manifest themselves as "natural phenomena" and then "in addition" signify something further; they are "symbols" for us. When we talk and think in such a way, we take it for granted that we know "the" sun and "the" wind "in themselves." We believe that earlier peoples and civilizations too "at first" came to know "the sun" and "the moon" and "the wind," and that they then proceeded to use these supposedly "natural phenomena" as "images" for whatever worlds lay beyond. As if it were not the reverse, that "the" sun and "the" wind already first come to appearance from out of a "world" in each case, and are what they are only insofar as they are poetized from out of this "world," although it may remain an open question just *who* is poetizing here. (See "The Wanderer," line 80: "Intimative mariners"; line 106, and the entire elegy, especially the conclusion.)

It is not the case that the "astronomical" sun and "meteorological" wind, which we of today believe ourselves to know in a more advanced and better way, are poetized any less than the "fire" in the poem, just less skillfully and less poetically. The poetizing of astronomy and meteorology, the "poetizing" explanation of nature in modernity is of the type that calculates and plans. Planning is also a poetizing of sorts, namely, the counteressence and privative essence of poetry. Even if the humankind of today and that which comes after it is technologized and armed to the extreme, anticipating a global situation in which the very distinction between "war and peace" belongs to those things that have been abandoned—even then the human being still lives "poetically" upon this Earth . . . but within the counteressence of poetizing, and for this reason without need, and thus also without access to poetizing's essence.

What Hölderlin thinks when he speaks of "fiery spirit" and "good voyage" must become clear in due course. For now, we should note only that the master key to all "poetics," the theory of "image" in poetry, of "metaphor," neither unlocks a single door in the realm of Hölderlin's hymnal poetizing, nor brings us anywhere into the open. Here it suffices to ponder only this one point: even the "things themselves" are already each time poetized before they become so-called "symbols." The only question that remains is in which essential realm and from out of which truth of poetizing.

§16. "The northeasterly blows." The favor of belonging to the vocation of poet

The northeasterly bestows favor and grace upon the mariners, those men of whom the fourth and fifth strophes of the poem tell. We must keep solely to what is said in these strophes, in order to know who the mariners are who are named here. The fourth and fifth strophes are already drawn into a clear connection with the beginning of the entire poem. Initially, we can only assert: "The mariners" are "the poets." The northeasterly is the "most beloved" "to me," Hölderlin says, because here he speaks as poet from out of his belonging to the mariners. The northeasterly is the most beloved to the poet, but not because it provides a personal sense of well-being or pleasure, or promises comfort. This "most beloved" belongs to the loving predilection of a genuine love.

To this genuine love belongs the shared willing of those beings that determine and thoroughly attune us in our essence, a willing that that which determines us be as it is. The word and concept "willing" and "will" fluctuate in their manifold meanings. In the willing that wills that the beings that determine us be, will does not mean a mere self-initiated, forcible bringing about of some wish that is itself reckoned upon. (On essential wishing, cf.: "The Walk in the Country," lines 19–20.[5] On essential willing: Fragment 25 (IV, 257): "Yet there comes what I want.")

Shared willing is rather a letting oneself go and releasing oneself into being. Shared willing is a having to, but a having to whose event transpires [*sich ereignet*] outside of mechanical compulsion, one that stems from an *open belonging to beyng* and returns back *into it*. This belonging, however, is the innermost essence of freedom.

The poet's loving predilection for the northeasterly wills only this: that for the poet, a belonging to what is essential, in this case, the "vocation of poet," remains. The northeasterly blows and swirls and carries the poet in the essential direction of that which he must fulfill. In the first line of the poem there resounds the good cheer that the poet is permitted to stand, and wills to stand, within the essence of that which first grants him his essence as his own.

§17. The "greeting." On the dangerous addiction to psychological-biographical explanation

Yet we can scarcely believe our ears.

> Der Nordost wehet,
> Der liebste unter den Winden
> Mir, weil er feurigen Geist
> Und gute Fahrt verheißet den Schiffern.
> Geh aber nun und grüße
> . . . .

> The northeasterly blows,
> Most beloved of the winds
> To me, for it promises fiery spirit
> And good voyage to mariners.
> But go now and greet
> . . . .

Does not everything here turn into its opposite?

"But go now and greet . . ." The northeasterly is released. The poet remains behind. He no longer seizes the favorable moment for the good voyage across the ocean to faraway coasts. He now "only" lets the land of the "fiery spirit" and the shoreline and the ocean be greeted. With this greeting the poet still thinks back to his previous sojourn there. The recollection of something past comes over him. This is, after all, presumably why the entire poem is called "Remembrance."

"But go now and greet . . ." Has the poet himself in the end grown tired of his voyages, exhausted and now taking flight into the mere recollection of something past? Does not this "But go now and greet . . ." indeed sound like the concluding strophe of the poem "Ganymede," which Hölderlin published toward the end of 1804 together with other poems in the publication, "Journal for the Year 1805, Dedicated to Love and Friendship"? It reads (IV, 69):

> Der Frühling kömmt. Und jedes, in seiner Art,
> Blüht. Der ist aber ferne; nicht mehr dabei.
> Irr gieng er nun; denn allzu gut sind
> Genien; himmlisch Gespräch ist sein nun.

> Spring is coming. And everything, in its own way,
> Blossoms. But he is far away; no longer there.
> He has now gone astray; for all too good are
> Genii; heavenly talk is his now.

"But he is far away; no longer there. / He has now gone astray;"—does this not, with an uncanny precision, correspond to the "biographical" fact that Hölderlin, following his return from France, was plagued by the onset of mental illness? What is more natural than for Hölderlin himself, in his long, lucid intervals, to have clearly experienced that what was now being demanded of him was the renunciation of his poetic being?

"But go now and greet . . .": Does not this speak of departure and renunciation, and do so precisely if the mariners refer to the poets, and the northeasterly to the favor and essential space of poetizing?

Already with this passage, and for the elucidation of the other poems as well, we must learn to see clearly. This means the following: we must free ourselves step by step from a comfortable, and, for this reason, especially stubborn and thus seemingly illuminating way of viewing things. This way of viewing things exhausts itself in considering a work to be grasped or even conceptualized when it is explained in terms of the psychological conditions of its genesis.

Now Hölderlin's poetic works from the period between 1800 and 1806 are obscure; their internal connections appear to be missing. Having said this, we know of Hölderlin's encroaching madness during these same years. The Hölderlin case is thus clear. No. Viewed in this way, it is not clear at all. For when seen from the perspective of this illuminating psychological-biological explanation of the work as "product" of "someone insane," the word of the work does not have its say, but only the presumptuous know-it-all attitude of those who are supposedly "normal" and not deranged. The poet was indeed deranged, in the sense of a de-rangement [*Ver-rückung*] of his essence, which was removed from the night of his era. This essential derangement then had as its consequence a "derangedness" that was certainly also unique in kind. Yet from this consequence, the ground can never be grasped. We must free ourselves step by step from our addiction to psychological-biographical explanation. Step by step, because it cannot be achieved by a mere change of "views." Nor does it suffice to discard our usual mistaken thoughts about Hölderlin.

§18. Norbert von Hellingrath on "Hölderlin's madness." Commemoration of von Hellingrath

In this regard, von Hellingrath already said what was essential in his lecture "Hölderlin's Madness." Von Hellingrath gave this talk to a small circle in Munich in March 1915 as the opportunity arose during a vacation; prior to this in February of the same year, he gave a first lecture on "Hölderlin and the Germans." The two lectures first appeared in publication in 1922. They were then published again in 1936 in the form of a "Commemorative Volume," put together by Ludwig von Pigenot with the title *Hölderlin's Legacy*.

In his lecture on "Hölderlin's Madness," Norbert von Hellingrath says the following:

He who lives thus among the gods, his speech can no longer be understood by humans; for the first time in Germany, poetic language ventures forth so undisguised, wholly from its native ground, grown in native air, however much the Greek model too was necessary to give the poet courage to create something poetically comparable. For this reason too, the Germans may be excused for not printing these great hymns or even reading those that were published, instead merely amusing themselves over the "traces of madness" that they found therein, with that comforting pleasure that reassures the petit bourgeois when, with official approval, he is permitted to call crazy one who is so uncannily great.[1]

---

1 Norbert von Hellingrath, *Hölderlin-Vermächtnis*, with an introduction by Ludwig von Pigenot, second edition (Munich, 1944), 161–62.

Rainer Maria Rilke was among those who heard the first lecture. An echo of this lecture is preserved in a letter that Rilke wrote to Norbert von Hellingrath's grandmother the following day (February 28, 1915):

> that Norbert's grandly formulated and sympathetic character of speech was indescribably gripping and meaningful to me; in looking at this monstrous world so fearlessly and purely and thus making it for himself into a visage encountered daily, he places himself into the circle of the greatest existence, into a spiritual expansiveness in which he can encounter nothing but great things. Where is there such a young man by whom one could be so reassured? I thought this often; yesterday, however, I became so strongly convinced of it, that the hour, in regards to his words, presented itself to me of its own accord as one of those that I have spent in the proximity of wholly redeemed, enduringly superior, spiritual human beings. It is gripping to see how a solitary human being, in that most decisive sense in which Hölderlin was solitary, can, for such a heart as Norbert's, become an educator, participant, and constant collaborator: so completely drawn in, so altogether integrated, dwelling together in such intimacy—and this from out of the remoteness of his ungraspable eternity.[2]

On December 14 of this year, 1941, it has been a quarter century since that day on which Norbert von Hellingrath died in battle as a field artillery observer on the front line at Verdun.

Through his work, Norbert von Hellingrath has been definitively admitted into Hölderlin's realm. He requires no glorification. It is only we who require admonishment not to become blind to the silent radiance of this figure.

Let us now listen to Stefan George's word commemorating his young friend:

NORBERT

Du eher mönch geneigt auf seinem buche
Empfandest abscheu vor dem kriegsgerät . . .
Doch einmal eingeschnürt im rauhen tuche
Hast angebotne schonung stolz verschmäht.

Du spätling schienst zu müd zum wilden tanze
Doch da dich hauch durchfuhr geheimer welt
Tratst du wie jeder stärkste vor die schanze
Und fielst in feuer erd und luft zerspellt.

---

2 Rainer Maria Rilke, *Briefe 1914–1921* (Leipzig, 1937), 37–38.

You more monk bent over his book
Felt abhorrence at the war apparatus . . .
Yet once laced into that raw fabric
All offer of protection proudly spurned.

You lateling seemed too weary for wild dance
Yet as the breath of a secret world passed through you
You stepped like every strongest into the trenches
And fell exploded into fire earth and air.[3]

§19. Hölderlin's de-rangement as entering the range of a different essential locale

Everything biographical and psychological is of no help to us in eluci-
dating the poems because the contrary holds: the biographical can first
receive its interpretation and be determined from out of the work. For this,
however, we must come to know the work in all its essential forms. It is
not only the elegies and the hymns that belong to the work from these
years between 1800 and 1806, but also the equally necessary translations of
Pindar and Sophocles. Common understanding certainly also has its own
illuminating explanations immediately at the ready here. One says: as a
consequence of his psychic disturbance, the real "productivity" of the poet
also diminishes, and this is why he could then only "occupy" himself with
the translation of other poets. Certainly a peculiar way of "occupying"
himself, when we consider these "tragedies" of Sophocles, and when, at
the same time, we come to know Hölderlin's translation, its extraordinary
character and its inner poetic necessity, and when, beyond this, we have an
intimation of what it means to "translate" here.

But even if all this should still be closed off from us and we were to persist in believing that this translating is only an evasion and side occupation,
then there is one thing that can teach us otherwise. That is the dedication
that Hölderlin placed as a preface to his translations, which appeared in
1804 under the title *The Tragedies of Sophocles* (cf. V, 91):

To Princess Auguste von Homburg

You sent me encouragement some years ago with a gracious letter,
and since then I have owed you a word in response. Since with us

---

3 Stefan George, *Das neue Reich* (Berlin, 1928), 117.

too a poet must do something else out of necessity or for pleasure, I have chosen this occupation because it is anchored in foreign, yet firm and historical laws. Apart from this, if there is time, I want to sing the parents of our princes and their seats and the angels of the holy fatherland.

Hölderlin.

We must recognize two things about this dedication: First, the plain-spoken decisiveness that is communicated here; and second, the unassuming superiority that veils hidden grounds and abysses within a genuine simplicity.

"Apart from this, if there is time, I want to sing the parents of our princes and their seats and the angels of the holy fatherland"; thus, it is not the "gods," but rather the "angels" that he wants to sing; it is not the fatherland as a present at hand political constellation that he belatedly wants to discuss with verse, but rather the "holy fatherland," the fatherland grounded in the holy, that he wants to poetize; indeed not even just this, but rather "the angels of the holy fatherland." It is not the princes that he wants to honor with verse, but rather their "parents," which is to say, it is the ancestors of the princely that he wants to poetize and their "seats," that is, the commencements of genuine sovereignty and power, in the sense that Hölderlin gives this word in his poem, "Nature and Art" (IV, 47):

> . . . und aus den alten
> Freuden ist jegliche Macht erwachsen.

> . . . and from out of ancient
> Joys has grown every power.

Much in the same way as the two letters to Böhlendorff, the dedication of the translations of Sophocles' tragedies announces the inviolable and essential certainty in which the poet's own poetic being stands. And yet this certainty remains separated by an abyss from the naïve fanaticism of a blind enthusiast.

Now is this dedication, is what is said here from out of an unfathomable plain-spokenness and solitary assuredness, deranged? Indeed—in the sense of a derangement through which the poet is now entering the range of a different time-space. This entering into the range of a different essential locale is, at the same time, an abandonment of the previous locale. Of this, and of this alone, does the line "But go now and greet . . ." speak.

§20. The "going" of the northeasterly. The "greeting" of the poet's going with it

The northeasterly is addressed, the wind itself in its "blowing." The wind blows in that, as we also say, it "goes." The wind goes in its coming. "The northeasterly blows" means: it is arrival. "But go now" also means: go on and go away. Perhaps. Yet in the first instance it signifies: Blow, wind, and be. "But go now" does not mean: stop blowing. This "But go now" does not send the wind away. It lets the northeasterly "go." The "going" is ambiguous: In going, the wind blows; in blowing, the wind remains. Addressing the wind holds it to its course, yet does not hold it up. This not holding it up lets the northeasterly be precisely the wind that it is. Holding it up, by contrast, would here be holding it still, destruction and loss. Everything that we force into mere subjection or into sheer pleasure for our sake, instead of releasing it into its own essence and letting it be elevated into the wealth of its essence, immediately withdraws from us and escapes forever.

"But go now" does not mean: abate and disappear, but rather: *be* the northeasterly, *be* "the most beloved." This "But," however, surely contains a clear contrast: Blow, wind, but go. Thus the line, "But go now and greet," is indeed departure. Certainly. But departure is not always "taking leave." Do we actually know what "departure" is? Do we even know what the "blowing" of the wind is, assuming that we do not simply mean the tangible movement of air? Blowing: a coming that goes, and, in going, comes. Departure is not mere release and empty remaining behind. Departure is also not a mere going away and vanishing.

The poet remains in the blowing wind in that he goes along with the going of the wind. Yet this going with the northeasterly is now indeed no longer the voyage. And yet the poet still remains with the wind. Going with the wind is now the greeting. Just as the blowing of the wind is a coming and going that reciprocally exceed one another, so the greeting is a remaining behind and yet a going with that reciprocally demand one another. To be sure, the greeting is sent with and sent along, and the greeting brings tidings from the one greeting. But the greeting is not a notification in which the one greeting gives a report of himself. To the extent that the one greeting speaks of himself at all, he says only that he wants nothing for himself, but rather turns over to the one being greeted all that is due to him.

REVIEW

"But go now and greet." This is renunciation of the voyage with the northeasterly as its wind, and yet is still a going with the wind. It is renunciation, but not the admission of an incapacity. It is departure. But departure is not end—it is perhaps sooner another commencement. The most beloved wind is not held on to. It is for this reason alone that what the wind brings, and the way in which it brings it, is also retained in the fullness of its essence. That is why the "But go now" speaks of a going with the northeasterly toward the southwest. The cardinal directions of the "sky" name the different "heavens," which are determined by the heavenly. What is heavenly of the different heavens must have differentiated and separated itself. Yet the separation is of a unique kind. For the poet's remaining behind under his heaven and in his most beloved wind is at the same time a going with it to that other stretch of the heavens. The going with, however, is greeting.

How often we greet, and with every good intention. What is more familiar to us than a greeting? What more is there for us to consider here? We could remain content with this familiar experience, were it not for the fact that the mystery of "remembrance" lies in this "But go now and greet," and if this "remembrance" did not—far beyond personal "lived experience"— ground something that someday will demand of us an "other thinking." For this reason, we must here know differently from usual what greeting is.

In the act of greeting we send a greeting. Greeting is, taken in this way, like the further passing along of tidings. Greeting and tidings present themselves as though they were something thinglike that can be passed along. However, the act of greeting does not consist in the transmission of a greeting thus conceived. The act of greeting is also not an announcing or notification. But the one greeting does, after all, announce *himself* in his greeting. However: the one greeting never reports something about himself in his greeting. To the extent that the one greeting necessarily tells of himself at all and in a certain respect, he says precisely that he wants nothing for himself, but rather turns everything toward that which is greeted, namely, all of that which is promised to that which is greeted in such greeting. This means all that is due to that which is greeted, as that which it is.

§21. Transition from the first to the second strophe. The greeting thinking-in-the-direction-of as the letting be of the greeted. The greeted thinks its way to the poet

That which is due beforehand to any being is the essence from out of which it is what it is. The genuine greeting is an address that grants to that which is greeted the essential rank due to it, and thus comes to acknowledge the greeted from out of the nobility of its essence, through this acknowledgment letting it be what it is. The act of greeting is a letting be of things and of human beings. Here too there are levels of greeting, ranging from the hasty, conventional and empty, to the rarity of the genuine greeting, and to the uniqueness of this poetizing greeting.

The act of greeting is a reaching out to that which is greeted, a touching . . . that yet does not touch, a grasping that yet never needs to "grip" because it is at the same time a letting go (see p. 72). In this way, the act of greeting always remains a will to belong to that which is greeted, and yet never takes the form of currying favor or of a calculative counting on one another. In the genuine greeting there even lies concealed that mysterious stringency whereby, each time, those greeting one another are on each occasion directed into the remoteness of their own essence and its preservation; for everything essential is, by virtue of what is its own, in each case unconditionally remote from what is other. Yet it is this remoteness alone that also ensures the moments of transition from one to the other. Genuine greeting is one way of such transition. The simplest and yet at the same time most intimate greeting is that whereby that which is greeted itself first returns to its essence anew, appears as a commencing, and finds itself as though for the first time. Only if we think the greeting in such an essential manner may we have some intimation of how Hölderlin, by way of the northeasterly and its "going," lets be greeted:

> Die schöne Garonne,
> Und die Gärten von Bourdeaux
> Dort, wo am scharfen Ufer
> Hingehet der Steg und in den Strom
> Tief fällt der Bach, darüber aber
> Hinschauet ein edel Paar
> Von Eichen und Silberpappeln;

> The beautiful Garonne,
> And the gardens of Bordeaux
> There, by the steep bank
> Where the footbridge crosses and into the river
> Deep falls the brook, yet over it
> Keep watch a noble pair
> Of oaks and silver poplars;

Who would here lapse into a clumsy and thoroughly inadequate manner of speaking? Who would here deform what is said so simply with additional paraphrases? We allow the greeted to stand on its own as it comes into view through the poetizing word. That which is said in the greeting does not, for its part, need our talking about it. We, by contrast, presumably do need a few hints. For this reason it is necessary to make this one remark, namely, that we should not mistake what is said for a "description" of something previously experienced. This is not a depiction of something actual; the "image" is too ill-defined for that. Much that could be described and that would serve to make a particular image complete is omitted. Or is it a result of this omission, that here, despite all indeterminacy, "the footbridge," for example, crosses by the bank as though it were *the* footbridge in itself? And why the footbridge, precisely?

This saying is not a describing only for the sake of describing. Nor is it some piecemeal weaving together of scraps of images and recollections. It is especially not an inability to compose ("bring together") a unified image complete in its fullness and lawfulness. Rather, the saying—what is said and how it is said—is determined solely by the fact that this saying is an act of greeting, and this greeting itself remains attuned by a fundamental attunement that is as yet veiled from us. In this greeting and through it, that which is greeted first rises up into its own magnificence and simplicity. For this reason, everything here is not just said differently; rather, what is made manifest in the saying is different from those places where poetizing is still permitted to indulge in a certain type of "description." Think of the fragment from the period of *Hyperion* that was not published until 1909 and, without a title, begins (II, 39):

> Komm und siehe die Freude um uns;
>
> Come and see the joy around us;

By contrast, in the poem "Remembrance," everything is said almost sparingly and yet inexhaustibly, everything almost forcefully and yet intimately.

If that which is greeted was actually to have once been like this, then it is, after all, only through this greeting that it is raised up into its actuality. What was once actual with regard to that corner of the landscape named in the poem has presumably long since changed—and yet—how much everything remains, how preserved, despite the indefiniteness of the whole, everything comes to shine. The beautiful river, the gardens of the town, the footbridge that crosses the steep bank, the deep falling brook—are brought together in the rapture of a *single* embrace:

> darüber aber
> Hinschauet ein edel Paar
> Von Eichen und Silberpappeln;

> yet over it
> Keep watch a noble pair
> Of oaks and silver poplars;

Oaks and silver poplars watching over river and town and footbridge. Here again we can only ask once more: Who would now want to touch Hölderlin's recollection and name what has been transfigured into this noble pair of trees and emerged into the pure illumination that their view presents? Here the act of greeting reaches into a realm in which "truth" and "poetizing," that is, what is actual and what is "poetized," can no longer be distinguished, because that which is poetized itself first lets the proper truth of what is true arise. The actual former landscape is now, by way of the greeting, poetized into this one that has been greeted. The greeted landscape, however, poetizes over beyond itself once more in the two trees into the transfigured and at the same time concealed site of a love that is no longer spoken, that has gone through a departure, and yet out of this departure still remains, an enduring love, over which the magnificent silence of these words lies. What they "think" has now been removed from everything biographical and taken back into the inceptual:

> Geh aber nun und grüße . . .

> But go now and greet . . .

Through the greeting, that which is greeted has first come into being. It now stands in the radiance of the poetizing word, stands and shines, so that the poet can henceforth think in the direction of what has now come into being, even though he is, after all, removed from it and must also concede this decisive remoteness, because it is precisely in this way that he remains mindful of that which once was and still now prevails in its essence:

> Noch denket das mir wohl . . .

> Still it thinks its way to me . . .

When is the "Still"? Now, when he greets, and in greeting addresses the northeasterly: "But go now . . ." This "now" and the "Still" refer to the same time, the time that we now already recognize more clearly as the time when the poet, having returned home from many foreign parts, remains back at the site of the origin.

This remaining back, however, is not like a being left behind and set aside. Remaining back is here not the lack of independence characteristic of some leftover that can no longer help itself and merely atrophies. Remaining back is an act of greeting, and the greeting radiates an intimacy that must come from a source of its own. What if this remaining back, instead of an uneventful being left hanging, were a *going* back, a *going* back to "the source" of the native homeland and to the inceptual that, in its thoughtful commemoration, is strong enough to sustain and to preserve what is inextinguishable in what once was and in the fiery spirit of the foreign?

Noch denket das mir wohl . . .

Still it thinks its way to me . . .

The poet does not say: still I think of it; he says the reverse: still it thinks its way to me. That which is greeted, in a thinking directed to the one who is greeting, inclines toward the latter. So mysterious is this greeting whose task is assigned to the northeasterly.

"Still it thinks its way to me . . ." is an interim word. It apparently interrupts the act of greeting and the tarrying alongside that which is greeted. In truth, however, it is like catching one's breath amid the fullness of the simple that the greeting northeasterly blows toward the poet, even though this wind goes away from the poet. Yet this is one of the mysteries of "thoughtful remembrance" [*An-denken*], which we otherwise call "recollection" [*Erinnerung*]. Such thinking in the direction of . . . [*Hindenken*] goes away toward that which once was and abandons the present. Yet in this thinking toward . . . , that which once was comes in the opposite direction toward the one whose thinking is directed toward it. It does so, however, not simply now to remain standing as a kind of presence, namely, as the presence of that which has come to mind. If we entirely leave to that which is recollected its essence and nowhere disturb its prevailing, then we experience how that which is recollected does not at all come to a halt in its presence upon its return, so as here merely to be a substitute for the past as something that still comes to mind. That which is recollected itself arches over beyond our present and stands suddenly in the future. It comes toward us and is still somehow unfulfilled, a buried treasure, although, when reckoned as something past, we otherwise count it among what is finished and inalterable.

The thinking in the direction of . . . that greets, giving itself over to the wind and letting itself be carried away by it, suddenly comes to stand in the wind that blows counter to this wind. It is as though a river that runs off and spreads out into the ocean suddenly flowed backwards in the opposite direction, toward the source. The thinking toward . . . that greets thinks of that which is greeted. Yet this thinking of it and thoughtful remembrance does not lose itself in something past. Remembrance is more mysterious in its thinking. Indeed, perhaps "thinking" is properly always "thoughtful remembrance." Perhaps thinking is something quite other in kind than that construct that "logic," as the "doctrine of thinking," informs us about. Yet it is from the proper essence of thinking that we may also first come to know the essence of "thoughts," and that means, what "spirit" is.

For it is not enough, and remains vague and undecided, when we indeed enthusiastically affirm what is "spiritual" and yet remain at the level of recognizing the spiritual as the "immaterial." For this in fact means only that we are measuring "spirit" in terms of material and ultimately conceiving it as a kind of "material," but just as one "thin as air." "Air," wind? Does not this poem also show a connection between the "blowing of the wind" and "thinking"? Certainly. Yet the decisive question remains whether we conceive of thinking as a blowing, and blowing as a wind current, and the latter as a movement of air present before us, or whether we place such blowing, in its coming and going, carrying and bringing, into a relation to poetizing and thinking, and comprehend the wind and breath of air and thus "spirit" too from out of this relation. Perhaps every "spiritual" [*spirituelle*] and "pneumatic" conception of spirit [*Geist*] is very un-spirit-like, and for this reason especially susceptible to the semblance of the essence of spirit.

In the poet's greeting, that which is greeted inclines thoughtfully toward him: "Still it thinks its way to me . . . ," so that he must give thought to it itself, yet indeed can give thought to it only in the greeting.

The poet's act of greeting is a "thinking"; the saying that greets, however, is a word of a poem, is a poetizing. What, then, if poetizing and thinking were the Same? But why then the different names? However things may stand, the attempt to "think" what is poetized in the poetizing is now already losing what initially impresses itself upon us and is inappropriate. Thinking is almost like a poetizing accompaniment.

§22. In the unity of that which is greeted, gathered by the poet's greeting, the day's work and stead of human dwelling arise

"Still it thinks its way to me . . . ." This interim word does not interrupt the act of greeting, but first draws the entire intimacy of the greeting into the word and "brings" all that is greeted "together" into its unity: everything, namely, that was previously named.

> und wie
> Die breiten Gipfel neiget
> Der Ulmwald, über die Mühl',
> Im Hofe aber wächset ein Feigenbaum.
> An Feiertagen gehn

Die braunen Frauen daselbst
Auf seidnen Boden,
Zur Märzenzeit,
Wenn gleich ist Nacht und Tag,
Und über langsamen Stegen,
Von goldenen Träumen schwer,
Einwiegende Lüfte ziehen.

and how
The spread of tree tops, the elm forest
Bows over the mill,
But in the courtyard grows a fig tree.
On holidays go
The brown women thereat
On silken ground,
In March time,
When night and day are equal,
And over slow footbridges,
Heavy with golden dreams,
Lulling breezes draw.

That which comes thoughtfully toward the poet from what has been greeted is now gathered with respect to the day's work and stead of human dwelling, which are shaded and protected from the all too harsh light and from the storm that tears through the broad tree tops of the forest:

und wie
Die breiten Gipfel neiget
Der Ulmwald, über die Mühl',

and how
The spread of tree tops, the elm forest
Bows over the mill,

We know from a late fragment, "German Song" (IV, 244), that Hölderlin there, and elsewhere too, speaks of the rustling elm in whose shade "the German poet" finds protection. A tree of the homeland casts its shade over the mill. Yet why the mill? Why is it distinctive among the steads of human care? The mill prepares the grain and serves the preparation of bread. In the period of the hymns, the magnificent elegy "Bread and Wine" is conceived in 1801 (IV, 119–125). Of this elegy, von Hellingrath notes: "It (the poem) will always remain the best foundation for penetrating into the world of Hölderlin's thought." The conclusion of the eighth strophe of this elegy reads (lines 137ff.):

> Brod ist der Erde Frucht, doch ist's vom Lichte geseegnet,
> Und vom donnernden Gott kommet die Freude des Weins.
> Darum denken wir auch dabei der Himmlischen, die sonst
> Da gewesen und die kehren in richtiger Zeit,
> Darum singen sie auch mit Ernst die Sänger den Weingott,
> Und nicht eitel erdacht tönet dem Alten das Lob.

> Bread is the fruit of the Earth, yet by the light is it blessed,
> And from the thundering God comes the joy of wine.
> Wherefore we think the heavenly too in this, who once
> Were there and who return when the time is right,
> Wherefore they, the singers, in earnest sing the wine god too,
> And not vainly conceived rings praise to the ancient one.

It is by no means because it also happens to crop up among the things that can be described in the vicinity and catches the poet's descriptive eye that the shaded mill is named here, but rather because the poet is commemorating the Earth and its fruits and those things that are of the Earth's provenance. (Cf. "The Wanderer," IV, 104, line 59: "Far off swishes the ever busy mill . . .")

> Im Hofe aber wächset ein Feigenbaum.

> But in the courtyard grows a fig tree.

The "But" seems to insert an overly stark contrast where we would scarcely think to look for such a thing. For why should mill, elm forest, and fig tree not belong harmoniously and uniformly together? This "But . . . a fig tree," however, following after the shaded "mill," reminds us specifically and once again that now the *southern* land being greeted and its fruit greet in turn. Elm forest and mill are also, and perhaps in the future, destined to this poet alone as his environment, the familiar companions of an abode in which the German poet nurtures his essence. Yet because the greeting comes from the ground of this poet's essence, this greeting is not some fleeting bringing to mind of something previously experienced that just happens to occur to him in passing. This greeting now belongs to the poetic being of this poet. For this reason, the one who greets must also beckon toward the wealth belonging to the essence of that which is greeted. The ground must extend into a realm where the intimacy of that which is to be decided, and can be decided only poetically, is safeguarded as though in a shrine. This is why the greeting blows and goes not only in the direction of land, to town and river, to brook and forest, and to the stead of human work, but to human beings themselves.

Part Two

"Holidays" and "Festival" in Hölderlin's Poetizing

§23. Preliminary hints from citing "passages" in the poetry

An Feiertagen gehn
Die braunen Frauen daselbst
Auf seidnen Boden,

On holidays go
The brown women thereat
On silken ground,

It is not just any human beings at some habitual hour who meet and reciprocate in greeting. "On holidays." Why do "holidays" occur to the poet's thinking? Is it because on holidays the women are especially adorned? However, nothing of that is said here. And why the women? Does the poet think of holidays because he is commemorating the "women thereat," or is he thinking of the women because he remains mindful of the holidays? Yet what is the point of these almost contrived and awkward questions? Why should the women not indeed be named in a "poetical depiction" of land and peoples? This surely makes the whole thing properly "lyrical" and gives it "atmosphere," and intensifies the impressions that the poem makes upon the "reader."

Whoever happens to chance upon this poem and is taken by this strophe may indeed find "poetical" satisfaction in the enjoyment of such impressions. Yet such partial sensibilities and narrow perspectives are irrelevant here, no matter how well intended. Our concern here is simply to know, perhaps in a purely extrinsic way initially, that "the holiday" and "the festival"—which are not the same—are repeatedly named in Hölderlin's hymnal poetizing.

Hölderlin's first hymn begins: "As when on a holiday . . ." Yet in interpreting this and other hymns we must first, at some length and frequently, seek to attain what is accessible, so as then, with regard to "holiday" and "festival," to properly—keep silent. It may thus be necessary to provide remarks on the hymn "As when on a holiday . . ." and at the same time to keep silent regarding the decisive word in the first line. Perhaps at the conclusion of this hymn certain individuals will think back to its beginning and then suddenly hear the word "holiday" differently, and intimate that the first strophe does not in the end seek to describe a mere image.

In our present undertaking with the poem "Remembrance" we must of necessity provide a direct pointer to what is meant by "holiday" and "festival." This can succeed only in a very questionworthy, because altogether makeshift manner.

We are told of "holidays" in the concluding strophe of the hymn "Germania" (IV, 181ff.):

> O nenne Tochter du der heiligen Erd'!
> Einmal die Mutter . . .

> O name you daughter of the holy Earth!
> Once the Mother . . .

(IV, 184)

And we are told of the "festival" in the thirteenth strophe of the hymn "The Rhine" (IV, 172ff.):

> Dann feiern das Brautfest Menschen und Götter.

> Then humans and gods the bridal festival celebrate.

(IV, 178)

The beginning of the hymn "Mnemosyne" tells of "holiday" and "festival" (IV, 225):

> . . . Schön ist
> Der Brauttag, bange sind wir aber
> Der Ehre wegen. Denn furchtbar gehet
> Es ungestalt, wenn Eines uns
> Zu gierig genommen.

> . . . Beautiful is
> The bridal day, yet we are uneasy
> For the sake of honor. For it goes frightfully
> Amiss, if One has taken
> Us too greedily.

These hints are questionworthy and almost embarrassing, because they follow the distasteful procedure of citing "passages" from poems that are here not even heard in their own right, as a word that is on each occasion singular and unified; it remains questionworthy, and even negligent, to "operate" with "passages" at all. Yet dragging in passages in this manner can perhaps arrive at what is most necessary and preliminary: that we now listen differently when in the poem "Remembrance"—which, moreover, comes from a later period than the three aforementioned hymns—we are told of "holidays" and of the "women."

"Holidays" [*Feiertage*] are "days of celebration" [*Tage des Feierns*].

REVIEW

Hölderlin's poem "Remembrance" begins as a greeting: "But go now and greet . . ." The four lines that come first in the introductory strophe are the foreword to the greeting. They name the messenger, the domain, and the path of this greeting. It is not the candidate for the office of priest, who was previously in southern France and for whom things did not work out there in his position as house tutor, who is greeting, but rather Hölderlin the poet. The greeting is a word of his poetizing. That which is greeted is greeted poetically. This is to note that that which is greeted and named in the greeting stands in an essential relation to what is being poetized in Hölderlin's poetizing during this period. That which is greeted is to be understood only as what is poetized in this poetizing, and that which is poetized here is in turn to be understood only as that which is greeted.

The greeting is by no means exhausted in bringing to mind and addressing the landscape previously seen, the human affairs observed, the human beings encountered there and their way of life. Nor does what is "poetic" in the greeting consist in the fact that what is mentioned in the greeting is "poetically embellished" to give a coherent image. Everything is more a piecemeal naming of almost random things and human beings, rather than a complete description of land and people. The telling that greets merely looks like description, and yet is something different.

What it is, we shall come to know if we ponder what is greeted, and how. Certainly, we shall never grasp that which is greeted by merely listing the things that are greeted. Whatever the greeting may name, that which is named is not told of as though it were simply brought to mind once more through the direction of the poet's thinking, thus merely through and for the poet himself. The reverse is the case: that which is greeted thinks its way toward the poet. From where remains unsaid. That which comes to be thought itself remains concealed. What if, in this coming to be thought, that which comes to be thought—"Still it thinks its way to me"—were itself greeting, and the poet were not only the one who greets, but *already before this* the one greeted? What if he were able to say this greeting only because he himself, in a still more originary sense, were struck by a greeting?

The interim word in the greeting, with which the second strophe begins—"Still it thinks its way to me"—makes us attentive to the fact that the *way* in which what is named in the poet's greeting is greeted, is unique in kind. Yet *what* is greeted is also more kept silent by the telling than made known; more kept silent, yet not completely, so that those listening can indeed in the end experience it, if, that is, they hear the greeting from its end in its full completion. The greeting comes to its completion in the second strophe with the lines:

> An Feiertagen gehn
> Die braunen Frauen daselbst
> Auf seidnen Boden,
> Zur Märzenzeit,
> Wenn gleich ist Nacht und Tag,
> Und über langsamen Stegen,
> Von goldenen Träumen schwer,
> Einwiegende Lüfte ziehen.

> On holidays go
> The brown women thereat
> On silken ground,
> In March time,
> When night and day are equal,
> And over slow footbridges,
> Heavy with golden dreams,
> Lulling breezes draw.

Differently from the preceding words of the greeting, the telling is here configured into a singular arc that enigmatically swings back into itself and in this way brings each of the individually named things to shimmer. The first four lines gather themselves with increasing density in the fourth, which consists of just two words: "In March time"; the ensuing four lines are like a relaxed exhalation in which the essence of this time brings itself to its unfolding. Yet what we would seek to point out in order to highlight the beauty of these words is merely the stammering of some external clambering around; one that is, moreover, perhaps premature, since we do not yet know what is said there. Pointers to what is beautiful are perhaps altogether out of order here, because the realm of art and of beauty, and all metaphysics, in which both of these find their exclusive site, is exceeded in Hölderlin's poetizing for the first time.

Some might also be surprised that these comments on the poem "Remembrance" linger so tediously precisely with the two introductory strophes, which are surely the strophes that are easily understood, because they can be directly intuited. The reason for the tediousness adhered to here is simple; it lies in the necessity of learning to know what is meant by "Remembrance." Yet only if we come to grasp how the poet in his greeting "thinks of" that which is greeted will we, from out of this "thinking of" [*Denken an*] that which is greeted, be capable of thinking the essence of "thoughtful remembrance" [*An-denken*] and thereby the poem as a whole.

The completion of the greeting begins with the line:

An Feiertagen gehn / Die braunen Frauen daselbst

On holidays go / The brown women thereat

"On holidays . . ." Why does Hölderlin, who during the period of his hymnal poetizing allows for no word to occur by chance or as a place-holder, name holidays precisely? Initially it may be sufficient to point to the fact that the first hymn, that is, the one that encompasses all those to come, begins with the words "As when on a holiday . . ." In conclusion we then noted, citing a superficial list of "passages," that Hölderlin during the period of his hynmal poetizing repeatedly names holidays and the festival.

Why are the "women" named together with the "holidays"?

What kind of days are these, the holidays? "Holidays" are days of cele-bration. And celebration?

§24. Celebrating as pausing from work and passing over into reflection upon the essential

"Celebration" means in the first instance interrupting our everyday activity and leaving work behind. This leaves us free for other things. For what? That is determined precisely by this "celebrating" itself, provided that all celebrating is not the merely negative act of ceasing work but rather emerges from the strength of its own essence. If, however, celebrating remains only the cessation and interruption of work, then the break that arises must be determined from another source, not from celebration and through it, but only from a relation to work once more. Celebration is, then, reckoned in terms of work, a means of relaxation and recovery by way of entertainment. "Celebrations" are then fundamentally in the service of work, ways of filling in breaks from work.

Strictly speaking, however, celebration, as the leaving behind of work, in fact receives its manner of being solely from out of the original essence of celebrating. We of today are scarcely equal to this essence any more, even though it indeed announces itself already in our routine celebrations. For celebrating, as a pausing from work, is indeed already a keeping to oneself; it is a taking note, a questioning, a reflecting, an awaiting, passing over into the more wakeful intimation of wonder, namely, of the wonder that a world worlds around us at all, that beings are and not rather nothing, that things are and that we ourselves in their midst are, that we ourselves are and yet scarcely know who we are, and scarcely know that we do not know all of this.

As such pausing, celebrating thus already brings us to the threshold of reflection, and thereby into the neighborhood of that which is worthy of question, and thereby once again to a deciding line. For it can now happen that in pausing from work, we indeed come up empty; do not know what to do with ourselves, search for substitutes; and right away our times of celebration have inadvertently become opportunities to take flight from ourselves and occasions for intoxication.

From the necessity of the unconditional priority of "work," "holidays," like work itself, then become either instituted or even abolished. "Holidays" are then institutions of human making. The essence of the holiday is in this way everywhere perverted into its opposite. Yet this corrupted essence of celebration only confirms its essence. For celebration is a becoming free from and relieved of the habitual through becoming free for the inhabitual of the day as the time of the festival, as distinct from night. The habitual here means the contexture of things and human beings that we constantly and proximately encounter and which, as a consequence of a well-worn way of doing things, we no longer appropriate anew in their own essence each time. The everyday then stands at our disposal from the perspectives of its utility, and yet in its essence it has not been authentically appropriated by us. The everyday thereby all too readily becomes the in-authentic for us. What is thus inauthentic no longer lays claim to our own essence; the relation between thing and human being becomes stultified in the routine. The world that has not been appropriated, the inauthentic, confirms, reinforces, and intensifies such habitualness. Things and human beings of the everyday world do not necessarily have to have this trait of inauthenticity and of such habitualness; yet they do so for the most part. They have it especially when the authentic dimension of things and of human beings has become inaccessible, when the inhabitual is closed off, when knowledge of it has been lost and care concerning it extinguished. This begins to happen at that moment when we come to understand care now only as worry and distress, as the effort of doing business and as the agitation of machinations, instead of recognizing that care is of another essence altogether, namely, obedience to the preservation of a belonging to what is essential in all beings—that is, to what is authentic, which is always the inhabitual.

The inhabitual, therefore, does not here mean the exception, the sensation, that which has never yet been there, but rather the contrary: The inhabitual is that which constantly prevails, that which is simple and authentic in the essence of beings, by virtue of which they maintain themselves within the measure of their essence and demand of human beings that they keep to such measure. The inhabitual can, therefore, appear and shine most purely within the habitual.

Celebration is a becoming free from the merely habitual through becoming free for the inhabitual. Celebration is an attentive listening to what Adalbert Stifter names the "gentle law,"[6] is awaiting the authentic, is preparing to appropriate what is essential, is waiting for the event [*Ereignis*] in which the essential manifests itself. The celebration becomes more celebratory not by the intensification or expansion of organized functions, and not by inflated grandiosity and the noise that attends its staging. The celebration is more celebratory when it comes to await more attentively the authentic festival. To the degree that a day is more replete with awaiting in regard to the appearing of the essential, it is, to the same degree, also a holiday.

§25. The radiance of the essential within celebration. *Play and dance*

To the festive there belongs radiance. Radiance, however, properly arises from the illumination and shining of the essential. Insofar as the essential radiates, every aspect of things and humans enters into the release of its radiance, and this radiance in turn demands of human beings adornment and ornamentation. The latter alone, however, never produce the radiance of celebration. The more festive the holiday, that is, the more it awaits the inhabitual in each case, the more all comportment is released from the habitual. The more released the comportment, the more vibrant and oscillating our stance. Yet the release of the habitual into what is authentically inhabitual is not an unleashed frenzy but rather a being bound to the essential and to the concealed enjoining and rule of beings. Being bound to the rule in free oscillation, and unfolding the wealth of free possibilities of what is rule bound, stemming from such oscillation—that is the essence of play. When the human being himself enters into play in the composed unity of his figure, there arises the dance. To the radiance of celebration belong play and dance.

The radiance of celebration as the radiating of the essential is not bound to the brightness of day; the celebration belonging to holiday can radiate through the night, which is to say: the holiday can not only last into the night but also can illuminate the night itself from the radiance of celebration. Here we are thinking ahead to the end of the fourth strophe of the poem "Remembrance." There the poet tells of a sojourn:

> . . . . wo nicht die Nacht durchglänzen
> Die Feiertage der Stadt,
> Und Saitenspiel und eingeborener Tanz nicht.

> . . . . where there gleam not through the night
> The holidays of the town,
> Nor the music of strings nor native dance.

It is never through the fact that dance and play take place that holidays arise and are. Rather, where a genuine celebrating is granted and this makes the day into a holiday, what is daily in such a day can swing into dance and play, thereby to maintain even in the habitual its lost radiance.

§26. The essential relation between festival and history. The "bridal festival" of humans and gods

Superficially reckoned, we may say that on holidays "festivals" are celebrated. Here for the most part we understand the "festival" in the sense of an institution corresponding to a sequence of official functions that the human being brings about. For Hölderlin, however, the festival has its own concealed essence. We equate "holidays" and festive days and festivals with one another and classify them within the time sequence of the calendar. The calendar is properly a festival calendar. Festivals are regularly recurring, sequentially instituted occurrences within a course of weeks, months, and seasons of the year that can be charted historiographically.

For Hölderlin, "the festival" is not an occurrence within the framework and on the grounds of history; rather, *"the festival" is itself the ground and the essence of history*. Therefore as soon as we actually begin to thoughtfully ponder this essence of the festival and of holidays, we stand within the decisive domain of Hölderlin's poetizing. We cannot evade the manner in which Hölderlin thinks history as soon as we want to grasp the essence of the festival. This opens up for the first time our perspective on an essential connection between festival and history that underlies the poem "Remembrance" and pervasively attunes all its telling. Thinking the essence of history, however, at the same time signifies thinking that history in which this essence of history itself became manifest as a defining truth. Thinking the essence of history means thinking the Occidental in its essence, and thereby thinking it from out of its relation to its first commencement, that is, to the Greek world and to Greece.

The two letters to Hölderlin's friend Böhlendorff before and after his stay in southern France were initially cited at the beginning of this lecture course merely in a "biographical" respect. Yet what they properly and solely tell of is the transformed essence of history that disclosed itself to the poet around this time. Admittedly, there is no direct or explicit talk of the festival in these two letters; and yet what is being thought of is only "the festival." A fragment from the period of the hymns gives us a hint of this (fragment 31, IV, 264):

         meinest du   zum Dämon
Es solle gehen,
Wie damals? Nemlich sie wollten stiften
Ein Reich der Kunst. Dabei ward aber
Das Vaterländische von ihnen
Versäumet und erbärmlich gieng
Das Griechenland, das schönste, zu Grunde.
Wohl hat es andere
Bewandtniss jezt.
Es sollten nemlich die Frommen
         und alle Tage wäre
Das Fest.

         you say   to the demon
Things should go,
As back then? For they wanted to found
A kingdom of art. Yet in so doing
They missed the mark
Of the fatherland and pitifully did
Greece, the most beautiful, perish.
Presumably things
Stand differently now.
For the pious should have
         and all days there would be
The festival.

We should not presume to grasp straightaway these fragmentary lines of a hymn. Here a pointer may suffice concerning the inner connection between the will to found a kingdom of art and the decline of the Greek world, between how things "Stand differently now" and the possibility of the festival to come. From this connection in turn, only the following need be explicitly emphasized: namely, that here "the festival" is named in a decided and manifestly singular sense. "The festival"—this word says something unconditional. The festival is not conditioned by the making of humans who by their own initiative "put on" and "stage" "a" festival somewhere at some particular point in time.

It is not through organizing celebrations that "the festival" arises and is; rather, all genuine celebrating prevails in its essence only from out of the festival and has its subsistence in the festival, from which celebration emerges in that it serves the festival. The festival is the ground of celebration.

"The festival" is for Hölderlin, however, essentially "the bridal festival" that "humans and gods" celebrate. "Bridal festival": the almost hesitant, poetizing word for festival. In this relation the word is already transfigured, and as transfigured is itself further transfigurative. The festival is the event [*Ereignis*] in which gods and humans come to encounter one another. What is festive in the festival is the ground of this event, which can be neither caused by gods nor made by humans. The festive is the inceptual event that sustains and pervasively attunes all coming to encounter one another in such encountering.[7] The festive is that which inceptually attunes. That which attunes in this manner pervasively attunes and determines everything as a silent voice.[8] It is the voice of an inceptual greeting through which humans and gods themselves first come to be greeted in advance. It is as those who are greeted by the festive, and only as such, that they—gods and humans—are first able, one and the other, the other and the one, to reciprocally also greet each other. What is festive in the festival, that which in each case lets the event of the festival occur, is the inceptual greeting, a greeting on the part of *that* which, in the first of his hymns—"As when on a holiday . . ."—Hölderlin names "the holy." The festival as bridal festival is the event of the inceptual greeting.

This inceptual greeting is the concealed essence of history. This inceptual greeting is *the* event, *the* commencement. We name this greeting inceptual in the sense of the coming of the holy, because it is first and only in this greeting that the encountering of humans and gods springs forth and has the ground of its source. The festival is the event of the inceptual greeting. Three things, however, belong together at once in this: first, that the holy greets, so that gods and humans come to be greeted; second, that gods and humans are thus those who have been greeted; and finally, that gods and humans, as those who have thus been greeted, ever since then have themselves greeted one another in turn, and in such greeting can hold themselves to one another. This holding and helping is a need. In his hymn "The Titans," Hölderlin enunciates the ground of this holding themselves to one another with the word (IV, 209, line 46):

> . . . Denn keiner trägt das Leben allein.

> . . . For no one bears life alone.

> (Cf. "Bread and Wine," line 66)

This word is valid not only for human beings, the "sons of the Earth," but also for the heavenly ones, the gods. In a draft for the late hymn "Columbus," we read (IV, 263, lines 37ff.):

> Denn einsam kann
> Von Himmlischen den Reichtum tragen
> Nicht eins;

> For of the heavenly
> There can bear the wealth in solitude
> Not one;

Gods and humans holding themselves to one another is grounded in the essence of the festival, that is, in the festive, which we must think as the greeting coming of the holy.

§27. The festive as origin of attunements. Joy and mournfulness: the epigram "Sophocles"

What is "festive" in the festival is not, therefore, thought here as a supplemental consequence or property, not as the veneer of the festival, but as the ground of its essence. If the festive, as that which inceptually greets, is the holy, then there prevails within the holy the attuning of an attunement that is always more inceptual and more originary than every attunement that pervasively attunes and determines us human beings.

Furthermore, we also find in nature an attunement in each instance. The thinking of modernity that conceives of the human being as "subject" and does so in a psychological and biological manner has fallen prey to the strange opinion, though at the same time understandable to everyone, that attunements found in nature are "naturally" only "imposed empathetically" onto things by human beings. This view is connected to the commonplace conception of attunements or "moods" that grasps them in psychological terms as "emotional states." However, the essence of attunement is of a different origin. We touch upon it with our pointer to what is festive in the festival. The festive is more inceptual than all attunements otherwise familiar to us and their opposites.

The festive is therefore also more originary than that which is joyful and most joyous, yet also more inceptual than mourning and supreme mournfulness. The festive is the ground of joy and mournfulness, and for this reason the festive is the ground of an inceptual intimacy and belonging together of both, joy and mournfulness. The latter is never merely the severed opposite of the former; rather, both, joy and mournfulness, correspond to one another, so that, thought in the direction of the essential, a joy always speaks within mournfulness and a mournfulness within joy.

Certainly, our thinking will never arrive at these relations so long as we regard mournfulness and joy only as the undulating rise and fall of independent emotional states that occur in human beings, instead of experiencing in a knowing manner the fact that in every fundamental attunement the voice of beyng speaks. Even if Hölderlin did not thoughtfully ponder the essence of attunement in such a way, poetically he knows very well what we have said and has also brought this knowledge poetically into the word, at the same time in relation to the supreme poetizing, that of Greek tragedy [*Tragödie*]. An "epigram" of Hölderlin's entitled "Sophocles" contains as it were the inscription in which this poet's conception of the essence of the mourning plays [*Trauerspiele*] is encapsulated.[9] The Greek mourning plays are not "theater" in the modern sense. They are celebrations and therefore oriented toward the festival. This now says: they are concerned with the relationship of gods and humans, and they contain and in each instance help to bring about a decision of the order of how a πόλις stands in each case within the truth of such an encountering of humans and gods. Hölderlin's epigram reads (IV, 3):

SOPHOCLES

Viele versuchten umsonst, das Freudigste freudig zu sagen,
Hier spricht endlich es mir, hier in der Trauer sich aus.

Many tried in vain to joyfully say the most joyous,
Here finally it speaks to me, here within mournfulness.

The most joyous within mournfulness? The figure and destiny of Antigone say enough. Yet does the converse also hold: the most mournful within joy?

Perhaps it does—if we think, in a sufficiently essential manner, the most mournful in terms of sorrow, and sorrow in terms of the essence of suffering, and if we do not equate joy with mere pleasure and merriness. Yet let us quietly concede that we know scarcely anything of all this. We of today especially are so devoid of knowledge here because despite the deprivations of a second World War, we are still incapable of experiencing the real need, which, however, not yet interpreted, the poet of this epigram suffered in advance.

Here, too, as often in this lecture course, we must forgo pondering Hölderlin's word in a manner befitting it. We merely draw specific attention to the "finally" in the second line. The "finally" names the fulfillment of something long-sought. And yet we would go astray if we were to think that Hölderlin, following a newly achieved insight into the essence of Greek poetizing, were henceforth intent only on imitating this Greek poet. The opposite is the case. Hölderlin, rather, experiences in the poetizing of Sophocles that which is other, that which once was, and this is why it becomes necessary to translate *Oedipus Tyrannus* and *Antigone*; this is why he wrests from himself the "Remarks" on the two mourning plays, "Remarks" that also belong to those hard to access treasures of which the Germans know nothing and are unable to know anything so long as they are of the opinion that they can find their own essence through their own invention, instead of apprehending it truly in the word of authentic history. Hölderlin, by contrast, in recognizing that which is other and once was with regard to his own history, and not in just any arbitrary foreign, at the same time catches sight of what is his own and to come. Hölderlin is able to write down the epigram "Sophocles" only because he knows the festive essence of the mourning play and the essence of the festival.

We are seeking the essence of celebration and of the holiday. If the festival is the event of the greeting of the holy, then celebrating has its essence in gathering itself around this event, and in such gathering releasing itself from our voracious and clueless confinement within the accustomed and habitual, so as to become free for the intimation of what is coming. If celebrating is this gathering that is an awaiting, perhaps indeed the radiant gleam of an indestructible, far-reaching forbearance and patience, then the essence of the holiday always consists in its properly being the eve or day before the festival.

REVIEW

An Feiertagen gehn
Die braunen Frauen daselbst
Auf seidnen Boden,
Zur Märzenzeit,

> On holidays go
> The brown women thereat
> On silken ground,
> In March time,

We are asking: what is meant by holiday, and what is festival?

Suspicions and objections have been raised that what is being discussed here with regard to festival and celebration is not to be found there at all. I ask in response: what is to be found there, then? What does it mean that this is to be found there in a text, and that is not? What does the researcher into nature see in the microscope? Maybe something correct, if he undertakes careful observation. But is the correct, which he sees there, already the true—that which lies before us and is to be found there and awaits us? It may thus seem as though here, too, in delimiting the essence of celebration and festival, we have merely proceeded arbitrarily, indeed violently.

To celebrate initially means: not to work. It may thus come about that holidays remain related only to workdays, that they are an interruption of work time, a diversion from the course of work and ultimately a break that we deliberately initiate in the service of work. Mere cessation is a negative kind of comportment. Some other arbitrary activity can be superficially substituted, as it were, to occupy the break, and, as we also say, pass the free time.

1. Celebration as becoming free in belonging to the inhabitual

Celebration as cessation can, however, instead of being a mere discontinuation and interruption, also begin as a pausing that arises not from a mere turning away from work, but from the human being's keeping to himself. Keeping to oneself is a way of coming to oneself and being a self in which one's own essence and its unfolding is freed up. Self-reflection and questioning then begin.

The suspension of work is now no longer the essence and ground of celebration but rather already the consequence of that keeping to oneself that seemingly directs the human being only back toward his "ego," yet in truth first transports him out into that realm within which his essence is suspended. Astonishment begins, or even a kind of terror. In one way or another, things become spacious, airy around the human being, without his already understanding this space and its expansiveness immediately.

The inhabitual appears. Its appearing does not require the enormous extravagance of the peculiar, or being incited by the unusualness of the latter. Celebration is now a being freed *from* what is stultified and habitual through becoming free *for* the inhabitual. The inhabitual, however, has its concealed measure in what is simple and inceptual in all beings. The inhabitual gathers itself in the fact that beings are at all, and not rather nothing.

Celebration as becoming free *for* the inhabitual is already a belonging to the latter in the manner of expectation. The steadfast insistence of expectation is awaiting. The more filled with such expectation a day is, the more directly it is a holiday. Times whose days are merely eager for the newest thing are without expectation, to which there always belongs reverence, be it only a glimmer. Conversely, expectation of the essential can pervasively attune us without our needing to eagerly count on what is or can be planned.

2. Improbable celebration in the echo of what is "habitual" in a day: the first strophe of the elegy "Bread and Wine"

Holidays are also not what they are through organized events. A genuine celebration cannot be brought about by making, because celebrating, in converse, bestows in advance the radiance into which the play of musical strings and dance ply themselves. From time to time, what is most celebratory in the most improbable celebration is that which, erroneously enough, we name the "echo" of a day in which perhaps "only" something genuinely habitual transpired. All this is brought into the word in a unique manner by the first strophe of Hölderlin's most beautiful elegy, "Bread and Wine" (IV, 119):

Rings um ruhet die Stadt; still wird die erleuchtete Gasse,
Und, mit Fakeln geschmückt, rauschen die Wagen hinweg.
Satt gehn heim von Freuden des Tags zu ruhen die Menschen,
Und Gewinn und Verlust wäget ein sinniges Haupt
Wohlzufrieden zu Haus; leer steht von Trauben und Blumen,
Und von Werken der Hand ruht der geschäfftige Markt.
Aber das Saitenspiel tönt fern aus Gärten; vielleicht, daß
Dort ein Liebendes spielt oder ein einsamer Mann
Ferner Freunde gedenkt und der Jugendzeit; und die Brunnen
Immerquillend und frisch rauschen an duftendem Beet.
Still in dämmriger Luft ertönen geläutete Glocken,
Und der Stunden gedenk rufet ein Wächter die Zahl.
Jezt auch kommet ein Wehn und regt die Gipfel des Hains auf,
Sieh! und das Schattenbild unserer Erde, der Mond,
Kommet geheim nun auch; die Schwärmerische, die Nacht kommt,
Voll mit Sternen und wohl wenig bekümmert um uns,
Glänzt die Erstaunende dort, die Fremdlingin unter den Menschen
Über Gebirgeshöhn traurig und prächtig herauf.

The town is quiet round about; the lane, lit up, falls silent,
And, decked with torches, the coaches rush away.
Replete with joys of the day, humans go home to rest,
And a pondering head weighs profit and loss
Well content at home; standing empty of grapes and flowers,
And of works of the hand the busy market rests.
Yet the play of musical strings sounds distantly from gardens; perhaps it is
A lover who plays there or a solitary man
Remembers distant friends and the time of youth; and the fountains
Still flowing and fresh cascade by the fragrant flower bed.
Quietly in the twilight air the peal of bells rings out,
And mindful of the hours a watchman calls the number.
And now a breeze comes too and stirs the tree tops of the grove,
Behold! and shadowing our Earth, the moon,
Arrives now stealthily too; the crazy one, the night, comes,
Full of stars and presumably little concerned with us,
The astonished one there gleams, a stranger she among humans
Rising mournful and magnificent over mountain crests.

3. "The festival" and the appropriative event. The festival of the day of history in Greece. Hölderlin and Nietzsche

Holidays are essentially holidays only when they are days of festivity, that is, days that are oriented toward the festival. The festival, however, is for Hölderlin by no means something that can be made or contrived by human beings, nor indeed is it any kind of occurrence that could also be recorded historiographically amid the course of other happenings. "Festival," for Hölderlin, is always "the festival." "The festival" is the reciprocal encountering of humans and gods from out of their essential ground. Such encountering does not consist in a mere "meeting," in which one party runs into the other and they run into one another, and do so within a time-space that is empty and contingent in relation to them both. In the encountering, humans and gods come toward one another from afar; and this afar is in no way something that is left behind them but is rather the space that they bring to one another in their encounter, without having found or opened that space themselves. Encountering is the reciprocal appropriation of their essence over into the essential space that first unfolds in its expansiveness and enters into its configuration.

What is inceptual in such appropriation is the appropriative event [Er-eignis] that already sustains and pervasively attunes, and thus lets happen, all encountering. The event [Ereignis] is history proper. Hölderlin thinks the festival as the essence of history. He does not enunciate this in such a form. Yet his poetizing springs from such thinking. The event is the festiveness of the festival. Here we are not regarding this festiveness as the consequence of the festival but as its ground. The festiveness that grounds the festival is the holy. And correspondingly: the holy in its historical essence is this festiveness.

The holy is beyond humans and "beyond the gods." Gods and humans, however, need one another. "For no one bears life alone." Because festiveness has its essence in the holy, festiveness is also more originary than the joyous, and therefore also more inceptual than the contrast between joy and mournfulness. Because both joy and mournfulness are grounded in something more originary—in the holy—they are united and are One within this ground. Because they are One in the sense of essential inseparability, what is most joyous can, and indeed from time to time must, express itself in mournfulness. Wherever such an event occurs is always the festival. Hölderlin says in his epigram "Sophocles":

> Viele versuchten umsonst, das Freudigste freudig zu sagen,
> Hier spricht endlich es mir, hier in der Trauer sich aus.

> Many tried in vain to joyfully say the most joyous,
> Here finally it speaks to me, here within mournfulness.

The "mourning plays" of the Greeks are festive celebrations. This means: here decisions are made concerning the encountering of humans and gods, and from out of such encountering. In this way, matters are also decided on each occasion concerning humans and concerning the gods. Festivals are the proper days of history, which is to say, history-forming days. For this reason, earlier festivals do not belong to the past but rather always play a role in preparing the coming decisions. This is why Hölderlin's predilection for Greece is not reducible to a scholarly or merely historiographically better-informed appreciation of "classical antiquity." Hölderlin's relation to the Greek world cannot at all be comprehended as a mere "predilection" that simply regards the Greek world as a model. And this is why, when speaking of Winckelmann and Lessing, of Goethe and Schiller, of Humboldt and Hegel and their relation to "classical antiquity," we should not name Hölderlin alongside them.

Especially erroneous is the juxtaposition of Hölderlin to Nietzsche that has recently become fashionable, despite the fact that it was actually Nietzsche who, already as a seventeen-year-old student at the gymnasium, recognized Hölderlin and gave him the distinction of being his "favorite poet."

This occurred in the context of a school essay from the year 1861, at a time when Hölderlin was almost completely forgotten among the Germans.[1]

"Nietzsche and Hölderlin"—an abyss separates them. In abysally different ways, both determine the most proximate and most remote future of the Germans and of the Occident (cf. p. 122).

For Hölderlin, Greece is the Other of the Western world. The one and the other belong within a singular history. The historicality of history resides in what Hölderlin names "the festival." Holidays, however, are the days *before* the festival.

§28. The greeting of the women. Their role in preparing the festival. The women of southern France and the festival that once was in Greece

"On holidays" there prevails the clear, unshakeable, yet also cautiously hesitant intimation of the festival. Hölderlin keeps silent concerning the essence of the festival, naming the festival the "bridal festival" of humans and gods. Because the poet's thinking is directed toward the festival, he poetizes in terms of the holidays and tells of the holidays. More appropriately and more cautiously, from our perspective we must grasp this connection as follows: that Hölderlin tells of the holidays indicates that he thinks in terms of the holidays, and that means: thinking the bridal festival. From out of such thinking he greets those who are most directly sustained by the intimation of the festival and are most intimately attuned to preparing themselves for the festival, and who find what is fitting in terms of the holidays and give birth to its radiance: the women.

This name here still carries its early resonance, which refers to a mistress or female ruler and protector, yet now in a singular, essential, and that also always means historical respect. In a poem that dates from shortly before the beginning of the period of his hymns and is part of the transition to that period, Hölderlin himself has said everything that we need to know here. The poem is titled "Song of the Germans." The eleventh strophe begins (IV, 129ff.):

> Den deutschen Frauen danket! sie haben uns
> Der Götterbilder freundlichen Geist bewahrt,

> Thank the German women! they have preserved
> For us the friendly spirit of divine images,

---

1 Friedrich Nietzsche, *Werke und Briefe*, Historisch-Kritische Gesamtausgabe, Abt. Werke Bd. 2, Jugendschriften 1861–1864, edited by Hans Joachim Mette (Munich 1934), 1–5, cf. 430.

The truth of these lines, still veiled to the poet himself, first comes to light in the hymn "Germania." The German women rescue the appearing of the gods, so that there remains an event of history, an event whose moment admittedly withdraws from any calculative reckoning of time. The German women rescue the appearing of the gods, bringing it into the gentleness of a friendly light. They remove from this event the terror that always leads us astray into the measureless, whether in the sensuous presentation of the figure and site of the gods, or in the comprehension of their essence. The damming, that is, damning, of the terrifying is, however, not a burying of the abyssal. To the contrary. Preserving the encountering of the gods in their appearing, bringing it into the gentleness of their image and countenance, however this preserving may be configured, plays an essential role in preparing the festival. The women are named because the poet's thinking is directed toward the festival.

However, in the hymn "Remembrance" it is not the *German* women who are named, but "the brown women"—this specifically recalls the southern land, where the sun's light is of intense transparency and its glow is overwhelming. The element of the "heavenly fire" here has a fieryness all its own, and the "exuberant genius" of human beings is here particularly exposed to this elemental power; it therefore needs to be especially regulated and shielded, so as not to be scorched in it. The encountering of gods and humans is different in the southern land. The festival has a different character.

When Hölderlin names "the brown women thereat," those of southern France, therefore, then they and everything in which they share, that is, everything that is greeted together with them, stand for the Greek world. That means they stand for the festival that once was, "in the land of old," where now no image of the gods that have fled is still able to shine ("Germania"). The letter to Böhlendorff of December 2, 1802, following Hölderlin's return from France, clearly attests to this (V, 327):

> The athletic character of the southern people, in the ruins of the spirit of antiquity, made me better acquainted with the proper essence of the Greeks; I came to know their nature and their wisdom, their bodies, the manner in which they grew in their climate, and the rules whereby they protected their exuberant genius from the violence of the elements.

It may now already have become clearer what the greeting "But go now and greet . . ." is properly directed to: not to what was encountered in terms of land and people during Hölderlin's stay in southern France, but to the festival that once was, to the encountering that once was between the gods that once were and the humans from the land of Greece.

Yet can someone greet that which once was? Surely the greeting can reach only that which still "actually" "is." Surely what is past is that which is no longer actual? Or is this act of greeting of such a kind that it first brings back into being that which seems no longer to be? Is the act of greeting exhausted in the sending and dispatching of a "greeting," or is the act of greeting properly a retrieval of that which is greeted, and not just any retrieval, but rather an exceptional one, a more inceptual letting arise? (Cf. p. 44 above). In general, is that which once was so definitively only that which is past? Is not that which once was distinguished from everything merely past and evanescent through the fact that, having once *been*, it still prevails in being? That which once was and has been is that which still prevails in being, albeit remotely.

As though to highlight this remoteness remotely in its presencing, Hölderlin names "the brown women *thereat*." "Thereat" [*daselbst*]— what "inspired" "poet" would venture to use such an unpoetic word as this "prosaic" "thereat," which for us today borders emphatically on the language of government officials and of business? Yet the poetic aspect of the greeting and telling of the entire strophe is so originary that any hint of the prosaic has melted away. Around this time, moreover, Hölderlin no longer shies away from words that initially come across as unpoetic and thus appear strange within the poetizing; for he has a clear knowledge of the fact that the more purely it resides within its essence, the more the invisible that is inaccessible to the senses also demands that which is altogether foreign to it for its mode of appearing. (Cf. "The Ground for Empedocles. General Ground," III, 317ff.) Hölderlin has now come to recognize that in a certain mode of poetizing, the "image," that is, what can be intuited in the presentation must be set over against, indeed separated from, the truth to be presented, in such a way that the presentation even denies that which is to be presented. The "sensation," that is, the attunement corresponding to the truth, cannot be grasped directly at all in an "image." Compare also the fragment "What is God? . . ." (Zinkernagel V, 149):

> . . . Jemehr ist eines
> Unsichtbar / schiket es sich in Fremdes.

> . . . The more something is
> Invisible / it sends itself into something foreign.

For this reason, Hölderlin in his poetizing chooses the alienating word, and this "thereat" stands in the midst of pure "poesy." This dry "thereat," however, draws together all that has been said into the unity of *one* world, to that world in which the brown women go *"on* silken ground" [*auf seidnen Boden*].

Linguistically, we might expect *"upon* silken ground" [*auf seidnem Boden*]. Because the handwritten basis for the poem is preserved only in the case of the final strophe, it cannot be decided whether Hölderlin composed the text just as it now reads, and whether, if this is how he composed it, we are not in fact dealing with a written error. If, as I assume but cannot directly prove, Hölderlin indeed wrote it as we now read it, then the accusative *"auf seidnen Boden"* instead of the dative highlights the direction. What is named is the ground not simply as foundational support of the going but rather as the emergent realm of the holiday procession, the ground sought out by those who are expectant, the ground over which they proceed, as the one suited to them and to their going.

Does the "silken ground" perhaps name the ground that is simply covered with such materials and carpeting, or is the ground itself "silken," that is, soft and quietly gleaming like silk, which is to say, precious and bearing within it, and yet bestowing, concealed richness? Does not the silken ground mean, rather, the Earth, out of which, and over which, and back into which there passes the breath of that indeterminate tenderness of the first, just barely indicated emergent stirring in early spring, containing everything at once: veiled indeterminacy and yet already intimate decidedness? The next line, consisting of just two words, relieves us of the answer to such questioning:

Zur Märzenzeit,

In March time,

Which time is that? The time of a transition. What is transition? We usually regard "transitional times" as "provisional," as "temporary" and thus passing, reckoned, that is, in terms of times that quickly disappear and are surpassed. Thought in this way, transition is merely a passing over; that which passes over is what is fleeting, without subsistence, not final, not decisive, something one must immediately get past as quickly as possible. Such is the calculative view of transition and of the transitory, that of a reckoning that is always in a hurry to put behind it whatever is momentary and to proceed.

Yet is transition just the hurried rush away from one thing that races over to something else and is thus neither the one nor the other but merely a continual "and so forth"? Is not transition also, and in the first instance, a passing over to the other side, in which process the side from which the passage proceeds is not then simply abandoned in the transition but rather brought with us in a peculiar way? Transition as going over and conveying a greeting?

The second strophe of the poem "Remembrance," in the consummation of its greeting, names the women. They are named because the poet is thinking of the holidays. He is thinking these because he is thinking the festival, the event of the encountering of humans and gods. The festival, thus understood, is the essential ground of history.

In the greeting, however, "the brown women thereat" are named. The southern holidays are meant. The southern land stands for the land of Greece. Greek festival, the encountering of humans and gods that once was, within the Greek world, is greeted. If greeting has its essence in letting that which is greeted be in what it is, then this act of greeting raises the festival that once was, as that which once was, into its essence. Why, and to what end, does this occur? Only to lose oneself in an inappropriate mourning over something past, to take refuge there, and furthermore, to forget the present urgency, and through this very evasion to act counter to and to be opposed to that which is coming? Why and to what end this greeting, directed to what once was?

Instead of pursuing this pressing question right away, we would do well first to see more clearly *how* the festival that once was is greeted, the festival that indeed is not even spoken of directly at all. We find instead only the depiction, without further "motivation," of a scenery that one might almost call "Romantic." So it seems, at least. Yet we may not assign Hölderlin's poetizing to either "Romanticism" or "Classicism." We must learn to see that such simplified classifications are perhaps very useful for promoting the business of science and for increasing the number of scholarly controversies, yet in truth remain an erroneous distraction. It then ends up looking as though Hölderlin existed only so that there could be scientific disputes over the relationship between Classicism and Romanticism and their variations and mixtures, and so that science, through such disputes, could maintain its "progress."

If we ask how that which is greeted is greeted here, then we are not asking about "poetological" forms or "stylistic devices" on the basis of some curiosity about Hölderlin's poetic workshop. We are asking in what respects that which is greeted becomes manifest in the greeting, and what it is, as that which manifests itself in this way.

That that which is greeted and the greeting are altogether simple in their essence demands a correspondingly simple hearing, as well. Because, however, we who are hearing, and are to learn to hear, have long since been entangled in all sorts of unexamined things, we are unable to apprehend what is simple in a simple and direct manner, without falling victim to essential deceptions through our regarding what happens to be commonly familiar to us as what is in fact simple. This is why the simplest lines demand the most extensive interpretive detours. Yet what is discussed in this process should never be misinterpreted as the attempt to impute some metaphysical system to the poetizing. The task of thinking that we are initially faced with here consists, rather, in thinking our way out of our entanglements in metaphysical ways of explaining. Admittedly, so long as poetizing is a hunting ground for scientific research, the path to the word will often be futile, even as the most extensive detour. For all "science" rests on metaphysics. Nevertheless, we must learn to hear:

> An Feiertagen gehn
> Die braunen Frauen daselbst
> Auf seidnen Boden,
> Zur Märzenzeit,

> On holidays go
> The brown women thereat
> On silken ground,
> In March time,

What time is that? Does the naming of this time tell us something about that which is greeted, insofar as the festival that once was is greeted?

March time is a "transitional time." "Transition" here does not mean that which merely passes by and is fleeting. "Transition" for us here implies *going over* to the other side, yet in such a way that the side from which the going proceeds is not simply left behind and thrust into oblivion.

§29. Transition as reconciliation and equalization

Transition thus does not mean away from one and off to the other but rather the essential manner in which the one and the other approach each other. Transition is not a passing over but rather a remaining that is gathered into itself, that unites the one and the other, thus letting both go forth from the enduring ground of their essence and letting them remain within that ground from the very first.

"March time" is a time of transition. It entails nothing violent or rushed, nor thrusts anything away. Everything, winter and summer, is as though reconciled within a concealed latency. This hesitant latency, however, is also not standstill but rather a singular arising and veiled emergence: reconciliation of the severity and brittleness of winter with the ease and strength of summer. Reconciliation is an equalizing; but equalization is not simply a making equal in the manner of a leveling out of everything into an empty and undifferentiated sameness. Reconciliation is also not the suppression and elimination of strife but rather a releasing of each of the parties in strife into the legitimacy of their own essence in each instance. True equalization places the parties in strife back into the equality of their essence. Equalization means that each is brought, in an equally inceptual manner, into the stillness of its essence and is sustained there, so that it may receive from this stillness of its essence the strength to acknowledge its counteressence, and in such acknowledgment also first to find itself fully. Finding oneself, however, is never a stubborn insistence on oneself alone but rather a going over from one's own to the foreign of the other and a going back from this acknowledged foreign into one's own. Equalization is going over and going back, is transition:

> Zur Märzenzeit,
> Wenn gleich ist Nacht und Tag,

> In March time,
> When night and day are equal,

Without saying explicitly what is properly meant, all the words here refer to transition and equalization in the essential sense: the time when "night and day are equal." We usually employ the word order "day and night." This means: we usually speak from the perspective of the day, as though it were what is "positive" and "night" the "negative." Hölderlin says: "When night and day are equal," and he does so not "for the sake of the rhyme," since this poem, like the hymns, does not know "rhymes." "Night and day" name the time-spaces of dark and light, of what is closed and what is opened, of the concealed and the unveiled, the far and the near. Yet all this in relation to the encountering of gods and humans, therefore in regard to the festival.

§30. "Night": time-space of a thinking remembering the gods that once were. Transition in receiving the downgoing and preparing the dawn

Night, for Hölderlin, is not simply a mere "image" for the absence of the gods, however; rather, night is the time-space of a quite specific relation to the gods and, above all, to that which carries and determines the encountering of gods and humans. Night is the time-space of mournful commemoration, of a thinking that *remembers* the gods that once were, yet are not past. Night is the time-space of a unique vigilance, one that may indeed be all too readily befallen by slumber and drifting off into sleep, without however being overpowered by the latter. The thinking that remembers those who once were, and who thus still essentially are, is oriented toward a remoteness; yet this remoteness is mysterious, because as remoteness it shelters within it at once that which once was and that which is coming. Each also refers at the same time to the other in each instance, and this especially when no decision has yet been made concerning either the remoteness of what once was or the remoteness of what is to come but where there is only remoteness. What is removed in such remoteness bears night within it; it is by no means something removed in the sense of eliminated, merely gone and away.

Night is not negative in essence. It falls into the semblance of the negative only if we abandon ourselves, without knowledge or reflection alike, to mere day or mere night. In truth, night takes over the evening's descent into dusk and brings about the rise of the dawn. Descent is not mere disappearance or coming to an end. Only something essential that is capable of entrusting itself to having once been is able to descend or go down in the historical sense. Only that which is great can go down; that which is small never goes down; it either continues on or simply comes to an end. Night takes over the descent and takes it into its safekeeping, for it is the preparing of the dawn. Night nights as night only when it is a receiving of the descent and a preparing of the dawn at the same time, and is thus the essential fullness of transition.

If, in March time, night and day are equal, then this is to say that the night, which precedes the day, has become ready to let the day and the coming of day take precedence in the transition, yet without relinquishing its other aspect, that of preserving for day that which once was. The essential equalization between night and day does not bring about the disappearance of both but rather brings each into its ownmost essence in each case, and brings both reciprocally into the unity of their mutual belonging.

"When night and day are equal" does not refer to some quantitatively determined, astronomical constellation, but is rather the veiling word of supreme, inceptual equalization. In night and day being equal in early spring, night is the purest transition to day, and day stands before the beginning of its ascendent rise. This equality is the summit of the pure granting of essence. This supreme equalization is the characteristic sign of the essence of the festival, of the event of the encountering of gods and humans.

§31. Gods and humans as fitting themselves to what is fitting. That which is fitting and fate

Certainly we are not to represent gods and humans to ourselves as present at hand entities that also crop up alongside others, so as to encounter one another on occasion within an empty time-space disengaged from those gods and humans. Gods and the human being are, but they are in the manner of fitting themselves to whatever is fitting. Here, however, that which is fitting by no means refers to whatever is in keeping with a prescription or rule, or with a custom. Hölderlin uses the phrase "what is fitting" in an essential sense. That which is fitting is, in the first place, that which is right and proper, in the sense of preserving a proper belonging to the essence. That which is fitting is, then, really that which is proper itself. Yet that which is proper not as some prescription inscribed somewhere that merely waits to be followed or not followed. That which is proper, as what is fitting, is that which disposes over whatever is right, ordering it in such a way that all that is to remain within the essence must order itself in compliance with this ordinance.

Fitting oneself into what is fitting is not simply a coming to terms with the inevitable. For that which is fitting is indeed precisely that which can be avoided and is even most often avoided. Fitting oneself to what is fitting means sending oneself out upon the path to one's own essence and toward finding the space of that essence, sending ahead one's own potentiality for being and giving it up to the favor or disfavor of finding what is fitting or not. This, however—sending oneself out into the finding or loss of that which is fitting, as fittingly sent and sending itself—this alone is what it means to stand within "fate."[10]

All too often we call fate "blind," only because we ourselves are blinded and miscalculate fate in terms of our calculations by regarding it as what is merely incalculable and "inexorable." It is certainly incalculable. Yet at the same time, incalculability is not an appropriate way of defining fate. If we encounter it merely as the incalculable, then we remain within the calculative attitude, even if we do not use numbers in the process.

Fate is the way in which what is proper, and that means, what properly belongs together, is fittingly sent into accord and equalization or else left in the realm of what is unequalized. Fate is, at the same time, the way in which those who are by way of expressly having sent themselves fittingly into their own essence, find and retain what is fitting, thus leaving to that which is fittingly sent and sending its essence, lending legitimacy to its prevailing, and so first receiving what is right.

§32. How fate is viewed within the calculative thinking of metaphysics, and "fate" in Hölderlin's sense

Our calculative thinking, yet perhaps in general all Western thinking hitherto since the predominance of Platonic philosophy—metaphysical thinking, that is—keeps to the single track of the sequences of cause and effect. On this track, all beings are lined up as actual–acting–acted upon. Whatever is not an actual effect is a cause, and vice versa.

The metaphysics that is determined by Christianity, and the Christendom that validates itself through metaphysics, think of everything in terms of its relation to a first, supreme cause that providentially determines in advance the course of the world and of nature. Characteristic signs of this calculative, planning thinking belonging to metaphysics are the concepts of predestination and providence. Within the framework of this thinking, fate either is regarded as a kind of cause that acts through providence in an unfathomable way, or the name fate stands for the effect of a cause acting in this way. "Fate" is then regarded by us as a cause shrouded in darkness, through which individual "fates" are effected. Thus, the word "fate" can also be misused to cover thoughtlessness and a flight from reflection, insofar as we content ourselves with registering that such and such is just "fate." That sounds grandiose, yet is vacuous and trivial beyond measure; it sounds like reverence, yet is perhaps only a helpless nihilism.

The essence of fate, however, does not consist in being an unfathomable cause of surprising effects. "Fate," thought strictly in Hölderlin's sense, is that which comes to equalization through the festival, and is therefore not necessarily that which has been equalized, yet nor, however, that which is equalizing. Thinking hitherto is without the adequate concepts and domains in order to adequately ponder Hölderlin's word "fate." Hölderlin himself names the essential domain and essential ground of fate when he says the word "intimacy" [*Innigkeit*].

The festival and fate belong together as one. From this fact alone, we can recognize how superficial our view remains if we indeed acknowledge fate, yet let it appear simply as a mere obscure power at the level of cause-effect relations. In truth this view is based on the idea that the human being is a being that can indeed direct himself and his own affairs within the sphere of a certain "degree of freedom," but for the rest is delivered over to the force of a sequence of inalterable cause-effect relationships. Within its own perspective, this idea of the human being is correct, yet the perspective itself within which the human being comes to be experienced in general here is woefully inadequate. The fact that metaphysics moves within this perspective and distributes all beings into the dual realms of the lawfulness of nature and freedom of the person (human and divine) must give us pause to think from the moment we perceive that freedom too is here thought only as a kind of causality; the interpretation of beings in terms of cause and effect, however, is, in the metaphysical sense, the technical interpretation.

The boundless domination of modern technicity in every corner of this planet is only the late consequence of a very old, technical interpretation of the world, an interpretation otherwise called metaphysics. The essential origin of modern technicity lies in the beginning of metaphysics with Plato. This modern technicity experiences its last metaphysical justification through that metaphysics that knowingly conceives of itself as the inversion of Platonism: through the metaphysics of the will to power that was thought by Nietzsche. The distinction made between the lawfulness of nature and freedom is in truth a technical one, and that means one in which being itself no longer comes to word from out of its truth.

If, by contrast, we think fate and destiny with a view to the event of the festival, and that means, if we inquire in the direction of that which grants this very event its essence, then fate indeed does not become more "comprehensible" to us in the sense of scientific explanation, but its essence becomes more richly esteemed and mysterious to us. Fitting oneself into fate demands from us something other than merely surrendering oneself to the inevitable workings of unknown causes, against which we—that is to say, our technicity—are powerless. In that fate requires from us something else, that is, something higher, it fittingly sends us ourselves into a more originary vocation and fullness of our essence.

§33. The festival as equalizing the while for fate

The festival is for Hölderlin the ground and essence of history. All standing within fate is historical. The event of the festival, as supreme equalization, brings all fitting of oneself, and everything fitting, and thereby fate, into an accord. The festival is the time-space and the essential configuration of the most intimate equalization, when each thing "is as it is." When each thing is as it, in its essence, is, then there is the true ("The Titans," IV, 209f., lines 51ff.; "Mnemosyne," IV, 225, lines 18f.).

In the festival the event comes to pass of that while in which fate happens for a while, insofar as whatever is fitting, one to the other, has found and fulfilled itself. The passage already cited from the hymn "The Rhine" more completely reads:

Dann feiern das Brautfest Menschen und Götter
Es feiern die Lebenden all,
Und ausgeglichen
Ist eine Weile das Schiksaal.

Then humans and gods the bridal festival celebrate
All the living celebrate,
And fate is
Equalized for a while.

Holidays are the days before the festival, the times before supreme equalization. Holidays are the night watch for fate. For a while, fate is equalized. Otherwise and most of the time, therefore, it is unequalized: humans and gods, and those who in their encountering interpret and prepare the fitting sending and what is fitting, for the most part do not find their way to what is fitting. We are therefore tempted to say: fate is equalized *only* for a while. The "only" then designates for us the limitation and restriction of duration, a lack of what endures, and thus the incompleteness of everything "actual." Already we are once again back to calculating and positing our self-serving desires as the measure of the while, of tarrying a while, of duration and remaining. We are all too fond of seeking authentic remaining within a continued enduring that never breaks off. Yet perhaps such endless "and so forth" is the most vulgar form of duration. Perhaps this kind of duration is habitually prioritized amongst everything desirable only because what has continued endurance in this manner demands nothing from us ourselves. Indeed, only what is habitual in the sense of used and employed, yet not appropriated, endures in the manner of an empty "and so forth." Not so the inhabitual, which is to say, the singular.

The singular also has its singular manner of remaining. It is that while of the festival that entails not restriction or lack, but the overcoming of all bounds of the habitual, and the wealth of the essential. Perhaps we stand before the distant vocation of "re"-thinking from the ground up a long-inculcated thinking that has become a calculating and sees supreme reality in the eternity of duration, and of experiencing the essence of being in terms of inceptual "time" and its while.

Perhaps this other thinking is a transformation, compared to which all "revolutions" sink to the level of the blind helplessness of the unleashed machination of a groundless humankind, because in their revolutionizing they merely go round and round and entangle themselves unconditionally in what has gone before.

Supreme and authentic remaining is not an enduring in a continual "and so forth" but rather the while of the singular. Yet that which is singular is "only" as the inceptual. Every commencement is singular. All continuation scatters into the multiple and leaves behind a multiplicity, and the latter always demands a going into what is scattered. This makes dispersion habitual. Such scattering can be combated, while retaining multiplicity as providing the authoritative measure, only through calculative accounting. What is dispersed and scattered also provides the opportunity, however, always to continue on and thus even to confirm the "and so forth" in its necessity and thereby lend it its singular legitimacy.

The commencement remains in its being for a while in each case, enclosing in such a while the inexhaustibility of the singular. The time of the festival is the while. For this reason, the day before the festival must already correspond to the while. The holiday is a specific whiling, attuned in terms of the festival and only from it. Such whiling is fundamentally different from the mere interruption of work. The time of the whiling is an awaiting, is already a kind of transition, is March time.

§34. *The transition from what once was in Greece into that which is to come: the veiled truth of the hymnal poetizing*

> Zur Märzenzeit,
> Wenn gleich ist Nacht und Tag,
> Und über langsamen Stegen,
> Von goldenen Träumen schwer,
> Einwiegende Lüfte ziehen.

> In March time,
> When night and day are equal,
> And over slow footbridges,
> Heavy with golden dreams,
> Lulling breezes draw.

"And over slow footbridges"—"slow footbridges"—"footbridges." We were surprised in the first strophe already at the fact that, among the many things that could readily be reported from the human landscape, precisely "the footbridge" and its "crossing" are named. And now we encounter "footbridges" once more, even in such a way that we are told specifically of "footbridges." Yet are we still surprised about the naming of footbridges, now that we know, or, strictly speaking, perhaps intimate that, and in what way, transition is being poetized here; passing over: "March time"—"equalization" . . . It would be vain and mistaken if we were no longer to be surprised now, instead of giving full sway to our astonishment over the fact that footbridges are named and what they are perhaps saying. "Footbridges" are now presumably no longer things for us that just crop up and happen to be mentioned among others; they are named as belonging to the time of holidays in March time. And this in such a way that they are named as that over which "lulling breezes draw."

"Breezes"? Did we not already hear of them? Of the wind, harbinger of the greeting? Yet now the "lulling breezes" belong to that which is greeted. Just like the poet who is greeting, that which is greeted is also within the domain of the breezes. Yet now they are "lulling breezes," not the cutting northeasterly that makes our eyes steadfast. The land being greeted is indeed another land, too, the land of Greece, in fact, where everything, and above all the ground of everything, the festival, is different. How it is, the poet who is greeting tells us, in that, in greeting, he lets that which is greeted be what it is. Yet that which is greeted seems to be such as to now demand a saying that veils rather than simply showing, in an unveiled manner, what is intended.

Once again, an interim remark is required here, so that we do not go astray either in hearing the poem or in its "interpretation." For we are now approaching the middle of the domain of the poetizing where our "interpreting" can least of all be brought to some result that we could record in a formula or in a proposition, so that, armed with it, we would know definitively about the "view" of the poet:

> Und über langsamen Stegen,
> Von goldenen Träumen schwer,
> Einwiegende Lüfte ziehen.

> And over slow footbridges,
> Heavy with golden dreams,
> Lulling breezes draw.

In the case of another "poet," these lines, if they were even possible there, might count as a "poetic description" of an "ideal landscape." Not so here, where something greeted becomes manifest through the greeting, so that it at the same time beckons over to the poet who is greeting. This entails: that which is named in the greeting, although it is said regarding the distant land, is nevertheless addressed to the one greeting, albeit in a transformed way.

That which is said has a dual, indeed even threefold, meaning: it refers to the greeted land itself and its history; at the same time, as that which once was, it refers by way of anticipation to the transformed manner of what is to come; and beyond this, and properly, it refers to the transition from what once was into what is to come. All of this is true not only of this part of this poem but also of the whole poem, indeed of the hymnal poetizing.

Yet this part of this poem is nevertheless distinctive. The lines sound like a floating indulgence in pure images and are like the tendrils on a rose that only by chance seem to wrap themselves around the authentic "content." Yet these lines here indeed enclose the authentic truth of Hölderlin's poetizing. Their concealed fullness—which is something purely simple and decided for the poet—this concealed fullness of the poetizing and its lucid beauty we may leave intact most readily if, within the bounds of our own capability, we ponder thoughtfully and soberly the individual words. They carry their poetic truth within themselves, moreover, and they do not require the vain attempt of wanting to intensify them via remarks. It is necessary to emphasize this repeatedly, so that we never fail to acknowledge the distance between the comments we are attempting and the poem.

REVIEW

1. The provenance of the poetized transition. The "demigods" called into the transition. Hegel and Hölderlin

Holidays are the days before the festival, and thus in truth the night watch for the festival. This is why the holidays are named together with "March time, / When night and day are equal." March time is a time of transition. Transition here refers not to that which merely passes by but rather to a going over to the other side. Going over is not mere departure but the receiving of a greeting. Transition is that in which the two sides that stand over against each other first find themselves in the back and forth and gather themselves in terms of their original unity, so as to receive from this inceptual unity their essential vocation.

Yet even when we think transition in this way, we still often fall prey to the danger of failing to recognize its essence. The reason lies in the fact that our thinking all too readily remains thinglike and takes refuge in the thinglike. For our reified representation of things, transition, as going back and forth, is then only something subsequent that mediates between two sides that lie present at hand, as though these otherwise subsisted beforehand and independently.

Thought essentially, and at the same time stated rather crudely once more, however, the following is true: transition is what comes first and first lets arise, in the process of going over, and from out of such going over, that from which and that to which it is a transition. For this reason, too, the transition does not float in a vacuum but is itself something that springs forth. Here, the bridge is not some thing that is installed from one bank already present before us to another bank that also lies present before us. Rather, at the very same time as it spans the river at a single stroke, "the bridge" arches over it, thereby first making the banks into banks and opening the open realm for a going back and forth. The greater the height from which the bridge arches, the more bridged and closer are the banks. Their distance from one another is measured not by the interval between two sides that lie present before us but in accordance with the height from which the span of the bridge extends.

The relations that hold sway here, and that are initially anathema to calculative, reifying thought, were already touched upon in our hints concerning the essence of greeting. There we said that those who greet can greet one another only if they themselves are already greeted, that is, already admitted beforehand into the bridge's oscillating back and forth, receiving their provenance from its span. Because Hölderlin thinks transition in such an essential manner, although not in the conceptual articulation attempted here, the transitional has a peculiar and intricate richness for his poetizing.

Transition is the encountering of humans and gods: the festival. Yet transition is also the passing over from the festival that once was to the festival to come. Transition is thus a transition of transitions. Within this realm of the transitional, therefore, what is everywhere essential is in the first instance the "between." Here are also those who, therefore, assume this "between," accomplish and sustain it, those first called. They are those who are no longer merely human yet are also not yet gods. Hölderlin names them "demigods." Their essence is configured differently in different times. Yet everywhere that Hölderlin thinks the realm of the holy, he thinks the demigods first of all and constantly; and he himself announces this in the hymn "The Rhine." The hinge on which this poetic work turns is the beginning of the tenth strophe, where Hölderlin says (IV, 176f.):

> Halbgötter denk' ich jetzt
> Und kennen muss ich die Theuern,
> Weil oft ihr Leben so
> Die sehnende Brust mir beweget.

> Demigods now I think
> And the dear ones I must know,
> For often does their life
> So move my longing breast.

In a variation that does justice to the essence of Hölderlin's saying "everything is intimate," we could also say: Everything is transition.

Transition is reconciliation, and reconciliation is that equalization which does not reduce things to being equal at the level of being without difference but rather imparts to each something equal, namely, whatever is its own in accordance with equal measures of its own essence in each case. With this elucidation of the essence of transition, if we regard everything formally and fail to ponder also that which is itself transitioning and its realm, we arrive in the proximity of the metaphysics of Hegel. The statement "Everything is transition" could be taken as a paraphrase of the fundamental proposition of Hegel's metaphysics. All being and every actuality is becoming—a proposition that recurs in Nietzsche's metaphysics, admittedly with a quite different meaning, and yet in the closest connection to the metaphysics of German Idealism. The attempt has indeed also been made to ground Hölderlin's poetizing upon Hegel's thinking, an attempt that immediately suggests itself when we consider that the two friends were close to one another in their thought and their will, not only while they were students but also in the decisive period of their maturity, during their Frankfurt years. Nevertheless, the same proposition "Everything is transition" has a fundamentally different meaning for Hegel than it does for Hölderlin; the difference does not simply concern two fundamental metaphysical positions; rather, the difference lies in the fact that Hegel's fundamental position is still metaphysical, whereas Hölderlin's is no longer metaphysical. The future appropriation of Hölderlin's poetizing depends upon correct insight into these connections, which has nothing to do with historiographical comparison.

2. What is fitting for humans and gods is the holy.
The fitting of the jointure as letting-be

At the point where our thoughtful reflection now dwells, we must initially think the transition, in the sense of the encountering of humans and gods. Transition and equalization, together with the "holidays," refer to what is prepared by the latter: the encountering of humans and gods, which is to say, the festival. Those encountering one another in the festival neither lose themselves in a blending that is devoid of essence, nor do they remain set in the rigidity of a mere opposition; rather, exceeding the encountering participants, they reciprocally impart to themselves their own essence in each case. This occurs in this manner, however, because neither humans nor gods are allowed to pursue or are able to effect the encountering of their own accord. Both are called to their encountering in advance, and indeed in a different way each time, by the holy, which fittingly sends humans and gods into their essential station. As that which fittingly sends in this manner, the holy is, for gods and humans, that which is fitting.

Such fitting configures the relations of the holy to humans and to gods, the relations of gods and of humans to the holy, the relations of humans and gods to one another, and the relations of this very "to one another" to the holy.

The unity and simplicity of these original relations is the jointure that configures everything and determines all that is order. The jointure we call *beyng*, in which everything that is prevails in its essence. The configuring of the jointure is a releasing into the essence yet at the same time unleashing into the possibility of the corruption of essence. Setting free is an admitting of disorder.

Fitting and sending are not effecting, and if we think them in that way, we are not grasping their essence. Yet let us quietly concede that we everywhere and always have difficulty in knowing being itself, instead of always only explaining beings in terms of beings along the lines of the cause-effect relation. We are always tempted to drag being as well into the reins of such commonplace explanation. While no longer knowing it, since the centuries when modernity began, the human being has been proceeding—and since the most recent times has been raging—through the world in a twofold entanglement as the supposed ruler of beings. One knot shackles our comportment and opining in the sense that we are focused only on beings and are estranged from being itself. The other knot entangles those who are thus entangled still further, insofar as the human being lets those beings, which he alone esteems, count as beings only if they are actual, that is, something actually effected or effecting, something that can be effected by him or at least explainable in terms of an effecting.

How should the human being here, entangled in this way, apprehend with a free mind and open eye the fact that something can be without it effecting or being something effected, that other things also are-with [*mit-ist*], without being effected by something else and, in being thus effected, exhausting being? How, given such entanglement, should the human being reflect on the fact that all being and being-with [*Mitsein*] is a being fitted into the order of one's assigned essence? That such order does not do anything, and does not occupy itself with beings, but that fitting happens in letting beings be? This letting and leaving provides the sign of the mystery that prevails here, the fact that fitting does not consist in effecting. Only if we ponder beyng slowly and at length is a light occasionally shed upon these relations. Yet much of this we can already recognize at favorable moments within the sphere of our daily undertakings and its little things. Sometimes we ourselves say that something is having an effect simply by its "being there" [*Dasein*]. Yet we still speak erroneously when we talk of "having an effect" here; the more essential point is that such simply being there is precisely no longer having an effect, and that in such no longer having an effect, being proper consists, in whose truth our being-with all beings resides, and from which it arises.

In the first commencement of Western thinking, still prior to metaphysics, which first begins with Plato, thinkers recognized something essential. It became clear to them that pure appearing and emergence is the true; and something still further, that even not emerging forth into appearance is capable of something higher within being than immediate appearing. Heraclitus, in a saying that is numbered 54 among his fragments, says the following:

ἁρμονίη ἀφανής φανερῆς κρείσσων.

The fitting of accord that does not release itself into
appearing is capable of something higher than the
fitting that appears.

We are thus led to take seriously the thought that self-withdrawal and concealing themselves let beings be more in being than does the activity of any causal effecting. In the letting be that goes away, the true becomes manifest. In the first version of his poetic work *The Death of Empedocles*, Hölderlin expressed this for the particular realm of being human. Hölderlin has Empedocles say this word (III, 149):

Am Scheidetage weissagt unser Geist
Und wahres reden, die nicht wiederkehren.

Prophetic is our spirit on the day of departure
And the true is said by those who do not return.

Within the sphere of the two-thousand-year dominance of metaphysics that has yet to be broken anywhere it must seem fantastical to think being otherwise than in terms of the guiding thread of cause and effect. We must attempt it, nevertheless, if we want to think ahead in the wake of what Hölderlin intimates under the names fate and sending.

3. Fitting as releasing into the search for essence and the loss of essence. Errancy and evil

Fitting is not causal intervention; it is not setting about the effective altering of what is actual. Fitting is rather the self-withdrawal and self-concealing that as such first lets beings be yet thereby also releases them into the discord of finding their essence and of losing their essence. Often human beings, while appearing to will themselves, roam around amid the loss of their essence. Often the gods show outrage toward the holy; often there is strife between gods and humans; often relations between the two are disturbed. Most of the time, indeed, everything wavers in its essence and is not in order; then beings get out of joint in their more extreme regions too. Everything out of joint brings confusion, confusion creates errancy, and errancy is the openness for maliciousness. With that which is out of joint, malice is set free. Evil is not that which is merely morally bad, it is not at all a shortcoming or lack in beings, but rather being itself as disorder and maliciousness. If order does not prevail, the fundamental ways of being, the elements, do not oscillate within the freedom of their essence. The ancient laws have become unhinged; they are no longer rightly plumb and level—that is, they are unright. This is why Hölderlin, in a late poem that has a concealed relation to "Remembrance," and that, left without a title, begins "Ripe, bathed in fire . . ." says the following (IV, 71):

> Aber bös sind
> Die Pfade. Nemlich unrecht,
> Wie Rosse, gehn die gefangenen
> Element' und alten
> Geseze der Erd. Und immer
> Ins Ungebundene gehet eine Sehnsucht . . .

> Yet evil are
> The paths. Unright namely,
> Like steeds, go the imprisoned
> Elements and ancient
> Laws of the Earth. And always
> Into the unbound goes a longing . . .

Yet if this is how things stand, and so long as things stand thus, the holy will still remain veiled, even in its concealment. Then fitting into one's essence remains absent. Then there is no equalization.

4. The temporal character of the "while," and the metaphysical concept of time

When the festival is, however, then fate is equalized for a while. To that thinking which reckons on effects and measures their actuality only in terms of their duration, the while appears as a brief duration. The while is reckoned as that which is merely temporary; it is disregarded as what is fleeting and without subsistence, in favor of that which lasts and endures. Yet the while of equalization is the time of the festival. This while cannot be measured by the clock. The whiling and remaining that is proper to this while is other in kind. We seek endurance in the habitual sense in the mere continuation of the "and so forth," which even considers its permanence to be attained only when it has renounced both beginning and end. Duration without beginning or end thus counts as the purest kind of remaining. From here, the two metaphysical concepts of eternity, *sempiternitas* and *aeternitas*, receive their hallmark. Yet just as "fate" in Hölderlin's sense cannot be interpreted by recourse to the cause-effect relationship, so too the essence of the "while" does not allow itself to be grasped in terms of the metaphysical concept of time prevalent since Aristotle.

That which is singular has in the while its appropriate kind of remaining, from out of the singularity of its inceptual essence. That which, within the perspective of reckoning, endures briefly, can indeed endure beyond every "and so forth" of mere continuation, namely, in the manner of an inceptual remaining that prevails in its essence *from out of* the commencement and *back into it*. The singularity of this one while has no need of recurrence, because as having once been, it is hostile to any repetition. The while of that which is singular, however, also cannot be surpassed, because it shines into and toward all that is to come, so that everything coming has its arrival only in the while of the singularity of what once was.

The festival is the while of fate that has been equalized. Holidays are the days before the festival, expectations thereof, and therefore already attuned by that while into a transition that tarries a while and is unhurried:

> Zur Märzenzeit,
> Wenn gleich ist Nacht und Tag,
> Und über langsamen Stegen,
> Von goldenen Träumen schwer,
> Einwiegende Lüfte ziehen.

> In March time,
> When night and day are equal,
> And over slow footbridges,
> Heavy with golden dreams,
> Lulling breezes draw.

Perhaps we now intimate why the poet must name the "slow footbridges"— the unhurried, simple transitions relating to the while, transitions that are not present at hand in some empty vacuum; for over them draw lulling breezes.

§35. *"Lulling breezes . . .": sheltering in the origin, the ownmost of humans and gods. "Golden dreams . . ."*

"Lulling breezes draw." To differentiate one domain, a sphere of tasks or a situation, from others, we speak of the fact that there or here a different wind blows. The different wind that blows here or there in each case tells us how things *are* there, the kinds of demands that are made on the human being, the stance that the human being must maintain there in order to survive and to do justice to beings; how he must receive beings and contribute something of himself or show restraint. The "blowing wind" thus names the different claims being made upon a particular humankind, and thereby also the distinction between what is assigned that humankind and what it brings with it. The wind thus names at once the distinction in the relationship between what is assigned and what we bring with us, and thereby the nature of what is given to a humankind as the task of its historical essence and as the manner of its festiveness.

Two different things are now named "breezes" in the poem: the northeasterly and lulling breezes. "Lulling breezes draw"—their draw and the direction of their draw belong to the land being greeted and determine what is proper to its humankind. They are "lulling" but not "putting to sleep" or even subduing in the manner of an oblivious sleep that forgets everything. The lulling indeed expresses the fact that here the human being is not putting himself forward and maneuvering within the realm of his own design. He is being traversed and carried by something originary, and thus brought into and maintained within that restfulness upon which his essence rests. Here, to lull is not to numb or in any way to deceive. To lull [*Einwiegen*] is to shelter in the cradle [*Wiege*] and keep sheltered there; it is letting be in the origin. The origin is for humans and gods their ownmost, that which they bring with them as their essence. Yet this ownmost is, at the same time, also that which is least of all and most seldom appropriated. Thus, it comes about that the human being is initially for a long time alienated precisely from his ownmost, and above all, helpless in the task of corresponding purely to the law of that which is his own. Hölderlin says in his letter to Böhlendorff of December 4, 1801: "The *free* use of one's own [is] what is most difficult."

What, for the human beings in Greece, is their ownmost? Which wind blows there? "Lulling breezes, heavy with golden dreams."

Von goldenen Träumen schwer

Heavy with golden dreams

That which is heavy weighs upon us and is a burden. Whatever is burdened becomes ponderous and even sluggish on account of its burden. Yet "heavy" cannot be meant in this way here. The lulling breezes, light, floating, enchanting, and playful, are heavy not in the sense of something sluggish but in the sense of something weighty, fulfilled, and full of promise. The breezes are called heavy because they are richly laden with golden dreams. Yet perhaps an excessive fullness and excessive weight of golden dreams is not even required; perhaps the latter are in themselves already that which is heavy, weighty, precious, and therefore that which can scarcely be mastered. The breezes that are heavy in this way are the distinctive sign of the wind that blows in that land at the time before the festival. These breezes carry with them the golden dreams in which the human beings of that land being greeted have what is their own, in which their essence is cradled, and in which it rests.

"Golden dreams." What is that—the dream? We are familiar with "dreams" and nevertheless have recognized little of their essence. The response to the question concerning the essence of the dream that we shall appeal to in what follows may not satisfy the demands of scientific, that is, physiological-psychological and psychopathological explanation of dream phenomena. We shall content ourselves with considerations of another kind, considerations that remain closer to the poetic telling of dreams.

However, we want to insert a brief interim remark that concerns not only the question of the dream but also every kind of scientific explanation.

§36. Interim remark concerning scientific explanations of dreams

Psychology and psychopathology provide definitions of the dream. Countless phenomena can be classified using these definitions. One can say, for example, that the dream is an altered state of consciousness. This statement may even be correct, although it would have to be asked what consciousness means here, and why the dream is classified under states of consciousness; why, and to what extent, the state of consciousness is decisive for the essence of the human being. Whether the interpretation of the human essence in terms of consciousness does not correspond to a quite specific self-experience on the part of the human being, namely, that of the human being of modernity, and this alone; whether one can in general explain the dream in terms of the workings of the human soul, or whether, conversely, it is not the dream that is instead conducive to first providing a view of the essence of the human being.

Simply listing these questions may be enough to let us note that the question concerning the essence of the dream is complicated and that the scientific explanation of the dream phenomenon is only ever of very limited help to us, because such explanations already rest upon propositions concerning consciousness, the human, the essence of the human, the essentiality of essence, and so on.

Must we, then, renounce the correct explanation of this line of poetry that speaks of dreams? Indeed, if we are of the opinion that the correct explanation is here and everywhere the psychological one, and in general the scientific one. Excluding the scientific explanation, however, is not a demotion of science, but only the acknowledgment of its limits.

Yet surely excluding the scientific explanation amounts to affirming an unscientific manner of proceeding? Certainly—if unscientific means nonscientific. Yet proceeding nonscientifically does not immediately imply an arbitrary and nonfactual mode of comportment within the realm of knowing. The nonscientific way of proceeding can, on the contrary, stand directly under higher laws than all science, even though it may often seem that, by contrast with the tools of scientific research, one is here appealing merely to direct human experience, or even only to the peculiar wisdom of language. The latter indeed help us more to find the path to what is authentic.

Those who take pleasure in such questions may try to figure out which is easier: to be trained in the secure apparatus of a science and to continue working within it, or to listen to the truth of the heart and to simply say it. The second is what is essentially more difficult.

In addition, we should ponder the fact that authentic scientific discoveries, that is, those that on each occasion bring about a transformation of science, do not consist in scientific observations, but have their essence in the fact that within a science, the courage to ask philosophical questions dares to arise. Where indeed the human being himself, not as a scientific specimen, but as being-there, is to be made the "object" of questioning, which is what "psychology" and "anthropology" claim to do, the kind of research that has been blinded by its own apparatus can indeed always provide a sack of results, yet without giving rise to any insight.

It may be permitted to cite a word here with which Stifter prefaced a tale from his *Studies*. It is found in a preliminary remark to the story *Brigitta* and reads:

Psychology has shed light upon and explained many things, yet much has remained obscure and very remote from it. We therefore believe that it is not too much if we say that there still remains for us a cheerful, unfathomable abyss in which God and the spirits wander. Often, in moments of rapture, the soul soars over it, from time to time the poetic art breathes life into it in child-like unconsciousness;

but science with its hammer and spirit level stands frequently only at the edge, and in many cases may not even have once laid hands on it yet.[1]

This was written around the year 1843; the position taken toward science is notable, because the conviction belonging to the second half of the nineteenth century is announced in it, namely, that "science" will indeed solve the puzzles, even though it stands only at the edge and has "not yet" laid hands on matters. From this still cautious "belief" in the key power of science there then arose very quickly, in the course of the following decades, that peculiar monstrosity that calls itself the "scientific worldview," the opinion that a worldview is only properly a worldview if it is scientifically grounded, which here always means in the first instance grounded in the manner of natural science and biology.

Following this interim remark we now return to "dreams," the essential definition of which seemed to demand of us psychological explanations.

§37. The dream. That which is dreamlike as the unreal or nonexistent

To recognize what the dream is, let us ponder that which is dreamlike. The latter becomes clear to us through two distinctions that diverge, yet are not entirely independent of one another. On the one hand, what is dreamlike counts as that which is unreal, without subsistence, and therefore null. Something is then a "mere dream." "Dreams are froth,"[11] something that floats fleetingly over the surface of what is real, something ungraspable and quickly dissipating. Here we are measuring the dream and whatever is dreamt in terms of the real.[12] Immediately the question stands before us once more: What is the real? We take it to be that which effects and is efficacious, accessible to us in its actual efficacy and ability to be effected, that which is graspable and at our disposal, namely, within the sphere of our own wakeful and calculative preoccupation with things and demands upon human beings.

Yet what is effecting and that which effects? What is "effect"? Is effect to be found only wherever we see a consequence, that is, something that follows whatever we have posited beforehand as that which brings about an effect and is effecting? Or are there also effects that are not consequences and do not require consequence? If the very boundary between one kind of effecting and another is fluid, then where does the unreal begin? And does everything unreal have to be already dreamlike?

---

1 Adalbert Stifter, *Gesammelte Werke in 5 Bänden*, Band 2: "Studien" (Leipzig: Insel-Verlag, 1923), 174.

We cannot offer a ready-made answer here. And yet the realm within which whatever is dreamlike may be thought makes itself known: The realm of beings and nonbeings. Admittedly, beings and nonbeings have been thought in different ways in the course of Western thinking. The fact that for a long time that which is in any sense effecting-effective-effected, that which is in effect real, is taken to be that which authentically is a being—this equating of beings with real effect—is itself one, and only one, among the Western interpretations of beings, yet it is the one that is predominant today.

§38. Greek thought on the dream. Pindar

In former times, and in the land whose history and festival Hölderlin greets, beings were thought otherwise, and nonbeings were therefore thought otherwise, too. Granted that the dreamlike refers to nonbeings as distinct from beings, and granted that in the poem the golden dreams are named in an essential relation to Greece, then it may seem appropriate to seek some advice from the Greeks themselves concerning how they thought the dream.

We shall undertake this, and do so on what is perhaps now the more appropriate path of asking not the thinkers of Greece, nor even doctors or those concerned with knowledge of nature, but rather one of its poets, and not just any, moreover, but that poet whose word became essential for a second time for Hölderlin during his hymnal period, and in a different way than on the occasion of his first encounter. For the purposes of illuminating the essential domain of the dream, we shall follow a word of Pindar's. It is found at the end of one of his late odes, the eighth *Pythian Ode*, 135ff.:

> ἐπάμεροι· τί δέ τις; τί δ'οὔ τις; σκιᾶς ὄναρ
> ἄνθρωπος. ἀλλ' ὅταν αἴγλα διόσδοτος ἔλθῃ,
> λαμπρὸν φέγγος ἔπεστιν ἀνδρῶν
> καὶ μείλιχος αἰών.[2]

Hölderlin himself translated this ode. We may initially adopt his rendition (V, 71):

Creatures of day. Yet what is one? yet what is one not? Shadows' dream are human beings.

---

2 *Pindari Carmina recensuit Otto Schroeder*, fifth edition (Leipzig & Berlin: Teubner, 1923), 245.

Pindar names human beings "creatures of day," and here he means creatures who are transitory and fleeting like the passing of a day: one-day creatures. Yet it is not immediately clear what the word ἐπάμεροι (Doric: ἐφήμεροι) means. Does it just mean that humans are "one-day creatures," of short duration? The creature of the day a fleeting creature. What does this mean, and what does it mean when thought in a Greek way? Inasmuch as the creature of the day is only something passing like the day, it still is in a certain way, and yet has also at the same time always already ceased to "be." One scarcely is, and already he is no longer, he is not. Whence the question: τί δέ τις; τί δ'οὔ τις: what is one, and what is one not?

Such a creature must be, yet at the same time also not be, it is a being and a nonbeing [*Nichtseiendes*]; yet if the human being *essentially* is also a non-being, then, as a being, he must also already be determined by nonbeing [*Nichtsein*]. Even that which is in being in him is not something that subsists on its own grounds or has steadfastness that resides within itself. Already that which is in being in him is not something arising of its own accord and set upon itself. Already that which is in being in the human being is not like that which emerges from out of itself, the light of the sun, but rather that which is *no longer* light, yet in such "no longer" still remains related to the light and proceeds from it, bestowed as a gift from the light. Already that which is in being in the human being is not a figure standing within itself and standing from out of itself, but only a derivative and descendant of that figure in the light—something deriving from the figure in the light and cast off from it, that which is cast by the figure in the light—a shadow (σκιά).

REVIEW

Lulling breezes, heavy with golden dreams, draw over slow footbridges. It seems to be almost trivial if we take the blowing wind on each occasion as a sign for the situation and stance of a particular humankind, for the demands it has to satisfy. Yet for Hölderlin, "the breezes" are something else. Initially we shall keep to the distinction between the "northeasterly" and the "lulling breezes" of the land being greeted. This distinction is often named around this period of Hölderlin's poetizing, indeed even in the elegies already, which directly prepare for the hymns. The distinction is that between the "fire of the south" and the "barren north." Yet the issue is not one of descriptively highlighting different landscapes but rather of a transition from one time of festivity and history to another—thus, of a "journey." This "journey" is, for the poet, the "return home." The return home from the foreign and from "colony" entails the task of an appropriation; indeed, in the first instance, of a finding of one's own by contrast with the foreign.

However, "the free use of one's own is what is most difficult." One's own we readily and in advance take immediately to be something secure; from such security there stems the haste with which we use and abuse what is our own. This semblance of possessing what is our own easily makes a fool of us and drives us around on the superficies of what is our own and prevents our appropriating it by the insidious ruse of letting such appropriation appear as something already accomplished. The foreign helps against this; according to a word of Hölderlin's, genuine spirit even "loves colony" (cf. the draft of "Bread and Wine," concluding strophe).

Being well traveled and experienced in the foreign has made the poet more experienced for what is his own. For this reason, the foreign is for him never something merely cast aside, it remains that which is greeted; indeed, in being greeted, it has the remaining appropriate to it.

At the time of festival and on holidays one's own, the ground of history itself, comes purely to appear; yet here, that which appears is not an object of contemplation. Appearing is a shining, in the sense in which, as we say, the sun shines. The breezes are lulling, rocking back and sheltering in the cradle, the origin. The origin and what is its own for the southern land have their essence in what is said regarding the lulling breezes. They are heavy with golden dreams. Heavy, that means here, fulfilled and rich with them, so that the "golden dreams" are, as it were, the center of gravity in which everything essential concerning this land, that is, its history, that is, the encountering of its gods and human beings, rests. The essential ground of its own for the land of Greece are "dreams."

What the dream is, we are attempting to clarify from what is dreamlike, in two respects. "The dreamlike" is, on the one hand, the unreal by contrast to the real. Pindar also seems to be thinking in this direction when he says of the human being that he is a shadow—indeed, a dream of a shadow. Pindar says this of the human being in response to the question of what the human being is, namely, as a "creature of day." Already the kind of question concerning this essence of the human being has caught sight of the essence itself; the question is already in itself of a unique kind, like every question that has genuinely arisen, as emerging from a relation to what is being interrogated.

Pindar asks: what is one, what is one not? This question by no means seeks to establish what the human being is in order then to supplement this with everything he is not; for there are many and various things that the human being is "not," and to enumerate all these would be meaningless and inconsequential. The double question means: In what does the being [*Sein*] of the human consist, and in what the nonbeing [*Nichtsein*] that is proper to him? In the double question there already lies the answer: to the being of the human being, there belongs a nonbeing.

To the question asking in what does the being, that is, in Greek terms, the presence of the human being consist, Pindar answers: In his being a shadow. A shadow is always cast, yet as this, it is also in turn something that sets in relief, that itself still gives a kind of view and thus shows how a thing looks: εἶδος. However, this "look" already no longer lets the being itself emerge, and for this reason the Greeks call the kind of view that shadows offer, and that they themselves are, εἴδωλον ("idol").

§39. The dream as shadowlike appearing of vanishing into the lightless. Presencing and absencing

Pindar does not simply say: the human being is a shadow. If that were the case, the human being would remain directly related only to the light. Pindar says: the human being is a shadow's dream. He says this of the human being insofar as he is regarded as a creature of the day. It would be equally erroneous, however, to assert straightforwardly that the human being is a dream. He is neither merely a shadow, nor merely a dream, nor merely both: shadow plus dream added together. The emphasis is indeed placed on the latter: ὄναρ, dream, but the dream is a shadow's dream. As something that sets into relief, a shadow is already no longer that which illuminates, nor indeed the light itself, but is already a kind of absencing on the part of that which illuminates and of that which itself properly appears. The human being: not that which itself illuminates, yet also not that which itself sets into relief, but a dream of that which sets into relief here.

What emerges from all this for the essence of the dream being thought here? Is the dream only an intensification of what is shadowlike, thus the shadow of a shadow, and thereby what is most fleeting of everything fleeting; a nothing, and therefore that which is wholly and utterly unreal? If we were to conclude this, we would miss the point of the Greek, for in naming the relation of shadow to dream, Pindar wants to say that the dream is the way in which whatever is itself in a certain way already lightless, absences: the dream as the most extreme absencing into the lightless, and yet nevertheless not nothing, but in this way too still an appearing: this vanishing itself still an appearing, the appearing of a passing away into that which is altogether devoid of radiance, which no longer illuminates. The shadow's dream is the fading presence of that which is faded, lightless; by no means a nothing; to the contrary, perhaps even that which is real—that which alone is admitted as real where the human being is stuck only with that which is constantly vanishing, the daily aspect of the everyday, insofar as the latter counts as the only thing that life knows as proximate and real. In the human being's keeping only to the mere daily aspect of things, to this disappearing

appearing of that which vanishes, he himself vanishes in his appearing, which is without its own illumination: a shadow's dream. Such is the human being as a "creature of day," who merely follows the whirl of daily events.

However, Pindar says not only this: the human being is a creature of the day, that is, of the everyday, and thus a dream of a shadow; Pindar says this word only as a prelude to another word:

ἀλλ' ὅταν αἴγλα διόσδοτος ἔλθῃ

Yet when the radiance, bestowed by God, arrives,
Illuminating light is there with men

καὶ μείλιχος αἰών

Hölderlin translates: "and delightful life" [*und liebliches Leben*]. More appropriately we must say, "and the world-time of gentleness," the while of equalization, that is, the festival.

Yet with this juxtaposing of the words concerning the human essence it only becomes still clearer that the dream and what is dreamlike, as altogether lightless, here stand opposite the radiance of the festival. The dreamlike is thus here, too, that which is not authentically real, in contrast to what is authentically real. What is the point, then, of this reference to Pindar? Is it meant only to give us a long-winded confirmation of what we too already claim to know when we say, "Dreams are froth"? Are we merely trying to provide ourselves with evidence that with the Greeks, too, what is dreamlike, as nonbeing, is measured according to beings? With this reference to Pindar's word, we fail to shed any light on the essence of the dream that could serve our understanding of Hölderlin's line. To the contrary, here we are, after all, told of "golden dreams"; dreams are here something that radiates, and this, moreover, is at the same time meant to characterize for Greek humankind what is their own. Instead of clarification, we merely create confusion. So it seems, if we only clutch at "real" results and definitions instead of recognizing possible paths of reflection and taking them.

What is dreamlike is supposed to be characterized according to two respects. On the one hand, in its relation to the real, that is, as that which is measured by the real. This characterization has now been achieved by us. At the same time, it appears to be superfluous. But we have not yet achieved it at all. For despite everything, we have overlooked what is essential in Pindar's word. What is dreamlike cannot be crudely [*globig*[3]]

---

3 *globig*: a spelling of *klobig* taken from Alemannic dialect. (Editor's note.)

and mistakenly notched up to what is merely unreal, or to the erosion of the real into nullity. The dreamlike and the dream are a vanishing of the light and radiance that itself is already absencing, of that which presences of its own accord and appears in shining (illuminating). The absencing, as the absencing of such vanishing, is also still a presencing. The relation to this presencing remains what is decisive in the dream, not the fact that it is a mere nullity.

Thinking in modern terms, therefore, we generally also think the Greek underworld, the realm of shadows, only as the realm of the unreal and null. In doing so, we fail to recognize the essence of appearing and presencing that prevails even here. The "shades" here are not a thinning out of something actual, but rather the independent manner of presencing of something that prevails in its essence.

Just as in the absencing of the dream there appears something that presences, so, too, conversely, there always prevails within that which presences an absencing. And so it is that what the human being is, as presencing in the manner of a shadow, he is not in the manner of mere presence and cropping up. There is nothing like that at all; rather, all presencing is in itself at the same time absencing. That which presences stretches itself as such—and not merely subsequently or incidentally, for instance, but in accordance with its essence—into absencing.

§40. The possible as presencing of vanishing from, and as appearing of arrival within "reality" (Beyng)

Thinking that is no longer Greek, and, above all, modern thinking, regards beings as the real. In the language of such thinking, what we have just thought through then sounds like this: the real essentially stretches into the unreal. There is no such thing as "the real" taken by itself at all. Yet the real is also by no means simply surrounded by the nonreal, as though the latter stood or lay merely next to it like an outer shell or sphere, just like the halo that the moon has around it. The nonreal is either the no-longer-real or the not-yet-real. The nonreal is in this way, and indeed in a different sense each time, the possible for what is actually real. The possible is in this instance never that which is merely null, or pure nonbeing; it is rather more a "state" between being and nonbeing.

How is this deliberation meant to help us in shedding light on the essence of the dream? To begin with, we can learn to heed the fact that wherever we measure what is dreamlike, as the unreal, according to the real, and in so doing judge it to be less real, we are already thinking erroneously; "the" so-called real itself already juts into the unreal, and actual reality is this jutting into the unreal. Conversely, the latter cannot be the mere negative correlate of the former. The possible reigns within the actual and real itself. Indeed, from time to time the possible is even more in being than the actual and real.

Let us for once measure—if indeed we have to measure—in other terms. Let us assess the dream not in terms of the real, which leads us to something null. If we assess the dream in terms of the unreal, and if we think the unreal as the possible that belongs to the actual and real, what do we then arrive at with regard to the essence of the dream?

Let us first think briefly of Pindar's word once more. According to Pindar's word, the dream is the appearing of a vanishing. However, that which has vanished is itself only one way in which that which is possible presences, that which can no longer be. Another way in which the possible appears, thus the unreal, as the dream was characterized, is the appearing of an arrival, of something making itself known in advance, coming toward us. This appearing is also presencing. If we once again think in modern terms, in the concepts of the metaphysics of modernity that were in currency for Hölderlin too; if we thus put actuality in place of being and nonactuality in place of nonbeing, then that which is arriving is neither something actual as yet, nor something merely nonactual. The possible as something arriving is a "state between beyng and nonbeyng."

Yet what is the point of all these deliberations for the task of clarifying the single word "dream"? In the interim you will also already have said to yourselves and asked yourselves: What, then, does this "abstract" differentiating and conjoining of the most general conceptual terms, what does this playing on the soundless strings of the emptiest representations have to do with Hölderlin and his poetizing? Answer: quite a lot, even everything, indeed.

§41. Hölderlin's treatise "Becoming in Dissolution." Dream as bringing the possible and preserving the transfigured actual

A short treatise of the poet's has been preserved from the period when Hölderlin's hymnal poetizing was in preparation; in von Hellingrath's edition, it comprises just seven pages (III, 309–316).

At the definite risk that all of us will scarcely understand anything of the treatise, I would like to read the opening of these few pages, and do so initially only with the sole intent of giving you an opportunity to learn to intimate from Hölderlin's thinking itself the realm in which his poetizing moves and from which its word arises.

If you come to see, on the basis of what is read out, that the interpretation being attempted here is by no means philosophizing too much, but rather in truth much too little and merely tentatively, insufficiently, then the point of this insight is not to make you agree more with the approach of this lecture course, but rather to make you more thoughtful concerning the concealed commencement of this most German of all German poetry.

Whoever is more acquainted with the conceptual language of the metaphysics of German Idealism, with the thought of Fichte, Hegel, and Schelling, may be able to find their way more readily within this treatise. Yet that does not yet guarantee a knowledge of what Hölderlin is thinking here. His conceptual language, too, is indeed not simply an outer shell but the appropriate articulation of his still metaphysical thinking. Hölderlin still thinks metaphysically. Yet he poetizes otherwise. This is also why a world separates him from Schiller's *Philosophical Poems*.

The treatise is titled "Becoming in Dissolution." It contains a reflection on the declining fatherland and on the essential grounds and concealed truth of this event. The treatise as it stands is a fragment, indeed the fragment of an immediate recording of the initial reception of the thoughts expressed therein, not yet given final form, yet on the other hand also conveying that confusing, unassuming freshness of what is manifest for the first time.

The fragment begins:

> The fatherland in decline, nature and humans, insofar as they stand in a particular reciprocal influence, constitute a *particular* world and connection of things that has become ideal, and dissolve themselves so that from out of them and out of the generation that remains and the forces of nature that remain, which are the other real principle, a new world, a new, yet also particular reciprocal influence may form itself, just as that decline emerged from a pure, yet particular world. . . . Thus in recollection of the dissolution, this dissolution, because its two ends are established, comes to be entirely the secure, unstoppable bold act that it properly is.

In what follows, there then stands the sentence that gave rise to our pointer concerning this fragment. It reads (III, 311):

> [in] the state between beyng and nonbeyng, however, the possible everywhere becomes real, and the actual ideal, and this, in the free imitation of art, is a terrifying, yet divine dream.

It would be presumptuous to want to understand this sentence taken out of context, if only because no one should imagine himself to adequately understand this treatise. Nevertheless, we can take from this isolated sentence a broad hint that may be of help for what we are attempting.

The becoming real of the possible in the becoming ideal of the actual is a terrifying, yet divine dream, and this in the free imitation of art. We recall Hölderlin's word regarding the Greeks that was mentioned earlier: "Namely they wanted to found / A kingdom of art" (IV, 264). Their history was to be grounded in art. In the said treatise, Hölderlin thinks the ways in which, within history, the world of all worlds comes to be presented, "set forth." In this setting forth there lies a constant corresponding to language, and that means, to the word proper, to poetizing, and to art in general.

In the free imitation of art, which is to say, in the founding that is accomplished by art, there is something like a terrifying, yet divine dream. What is the role of the dreamlike here, where the issue is the founding of a kingdom, the grounding of history? The dreamlike cannot here refer to the unreal in the sense of mere vanishing and nonbeing; to the contrary: the dreamlike concerns the becoming real of the possible in the becoming ideal of the actual. The actual recedes into recollection as the possible, namely, as that which is coming, binds our expectation. This taken as one, wherever art founds history, is a dream. The dream brings the not yet appropriated fullness of the possible and preserves the transfigured recollection of the actual.

In the poem, the dreams are called golden—that is, heavy from the integrity of the essential; golden—that is, radiating from the preciousness of the approaching gift; golden—that is, noble from the purity of what is here decided. These dreams that sustain art are terrifying, yet divine. Terrifying, because they arise out of humankind like something foreign and disconcerting and yet as one's ownmost, filling the ether (the air) in which humankind finds its essence; yet at the same time divine—because they call humankind into an encountering with the gods and show that which is one's own and terrifying to be neither something that merely grows from a nature proliferating in isolation and simply present at hand, nor indeed a product of, or something made by, human beings.

That which is one's own, coming from birth and laid in the cradle, is protected by the lulling breezes, heavy with golden dreams. The dreams here are not that which is vanishing and unreal in relation to the real; they themselves, if we are to think in terms of this distinction for the moment, are what is real, that which is more in being and more filled with being than whatever is merely picked up and consumable, in use without art. Such things, which are exhausted and worn out in being readily available for exploitation, while yet remaining recalcitrant, are the unreal. That which is "dreamlike" now signifies the opposite; dreams are not now "froth," but rather the wave itself, the ocean itself—the very element. The golden dreams—the radiance of their fiery glow—fill the element, the ether, the breezes in which the Greek people's ownmost "life" breathes. The fire and the fiery is their ownmost, the free use of which was once what was most difficult for that humankind.

That which radiates in the glow of these dreams, the poet does not say. Almost as though it were enough for the fire of the golden dreams to glow and radiate and serve to attune the vocation of art.

Part Three

The Search for the Free Use of One's Own

§42. Hesitant awe before the transition onto "slow footbridges"

To be able to make free use of one's ownmost, to first of all be capable of learning the free use of one's own, admittedly requires a confrontation with the foreign. Spirit must therefore venture into the foreign, not to get lost there and fail to attain what belongs to the fatherland, but presumably to make itself ready and strong in the foreign for what is its own, for this will not let itself be appropriated by a sudden assault upon what is supposedly one's own. One's own does not let itself be attained by a violent and at the same time compulsive commandeering of one's own kind, as though the latter could be identified like some scientifically ascertainable fact. One's own does not let itself be proclaimed like a dogma whose stipulations can be enacted in accordance with some prescription. One's own is what is most difficult to find, and therefore easiest to miss. This happened even to the Greeks (IV, 264):

> Nemlich sie wollten stiften
> Ein Reich der Kunst. Dabei ward aber
> Das Vaterländische von ihnen
> Versäumet und erbärmlich gieng
> Das Griechenland, das schönste, zu Grunde.

> For they wanted to found
> A kingdom of art. Yet in so doing
> They missed the mark
> Of the fatherland and pitifully did
> Greece, the most beautiful, perish.

That which is most difficult to find, as is one's own and nearest, must be sought for the longest time, and so long as it is being sought, it is never lost. All rushed and overhasty seeking is not seeking, but rather only a confused and errant wandering from one thing to another. To seeking there belongs the steadfast pause for reflection. Reflection is like awe's catching its breath before an anticipated miracle. Genuine seeking is a steadfast hesitating. Not the hesitation of one who is merely clueless and indecisive, but rather the hesitation of one who tarries long, who looks back and looks ahead, because he is seeking and tarries within the transition. The finding and appropriation of one's own is one with the hesitancy of transition.

Named together with one's own, with the "lulling breezes heavy with golden dreams," are the "slow footbridges." Footbridges are the inconspicuous bridges; so inconspicuous because they belong to that between which they are a transition. The footbridge is almost as though it has originated together with moss and reeds, with alders and birch trees, with brook and rocks. Footbridges, in their inconspicuousness and origination, are at the same time narrow bridges, only ever for the few individuals who have come to be at home amid the inconspicuous and that which emerges in an inceptual manner. The slow footbridges and the lulling breezes are not two separate things within some random landscape. The breezes draw over across slow footbridges, and the footbridges form the transition simply and decisively in the drawing of the breezes.

The span of these bridges appears to be lacking, since, after all, they lead straight and level from one bank to another. Yet their span is not lacking. It is merely concealed and higher than the span of any broad and sweeping bridge that anyone and all the masses can hasten over. The height of the footbridges' span is determined in terms of the height of the drawing breezes, in terms of the essentialness of the golden freight that they carry.

Hesitant awe is proper to the holidays that precede the festival. Hesitation and awe are necessary for every festival and in every transition.[13]

In the consummation of the greeting there stands the word concerning the "slow footbridges," not only because the festival that was once in the land of Greece is being greeted, but also because this greeting itself is intrinsically transition. The poet's own saying, his poetizing and being a poet, must go over a footbridge; indeed, it is itself only a slow footbridge. "Only"—that does not mean limitation, but rather the fullness of the singular and simple that can be none other than beyng itself, which here in the poetizing unveils its truth as it conceals it.

We experience something of this footbridge if, in the poem "Remembrance," we accomplish the transition from the first two strophes, which have now been elucidated, to the third and following strophes.

REVIEW

Pindar's word concerning the human being, found in one of his late odes, was meant to prod us in the direction in which we must think the essence of the dream and the dreamlike. In doing so, we leave aside all psychological and physiological explanations, for these necessarily grope in the dark if the kind of being pertaining to what is dreamt and dreamlike has not been clarified beforehand. This can happen, however, only by our contrasting the kind of being pertaining to the dreamlike with those beings that are more familiar to us. Keeping with the manner of thinking belonging to modernity, we call these familiar beings the real. Measured by them, the dreamlike is what is merely unreal and null.

If, however, we think through in a Greek manner Pindar's word concerning the human being, that, as a creature of the everyday, he is σκιᾶς ὄναρ, a shadow's dream, then we come to recognize that what is dreamlike is also a way of presencing, that is, of being, one that is proper to it—namely, the presencing of absencing, of shadow, which for its part already rests in an absencing of that which illuminates. Even that which is absent, more clearly, that which prevails as away, comes forth into presence. What is dreamlike, therefore, because it comes to presence, is not straightforwardly the unreal as opposed to the real.

Conversely, however, it is also the case that that which presences prevails as away, and so what is real juts into the unreal. If the real and actual is that which has been effected by an effecting, and effecting is a coming to be, then this entails an away-from-something in moving-toward-something. There is no such thing at all as something merely real and actual taken by itself. Everything actual juts into the possible, whether this now signifies the not yet actual or the no longer actual. Such jutting into the possible belongs to actuality itself and is not, for instance, some addition that is added on to what is otherwise already actual. Precisely this "otherwise already actual" does not exist. What emerges from this is the following: even if we measure the dreamlike according to the actual, this can take place only in such a way that we think the actual in its full actuality, and thus take into account its essential character of possibility. But if the dreamlike is something unreal, nonactual, what then—does it not then belong to the actual? Is not what emerges from this the directive to think the dreamlike in terms of the unreal or nonactual in its relation to the "real" or "actual"? In the fragment of Hölderlin's treatise "Becoming in Dissolution," we come upon connections that shed light on the essence of the dreamlike, insofar as it is thought as unreal, and that means, as something possible:

> [in] the state between beyng and nonbeyng [i.e., in the transition, therefore], however, the possible everywhere becomes real, and the actual ideal, and this, in the free imitation of art, is a terrifying, yet divine dream.

Here the dream is named in connection with a depiction of what is essential regarding history, and that is its transitions. The possible is here thought in its actualization, namely, in such a way that what was hitherto actual becomes ideal and presences in recollection. The dream and dreams are something that comes, and not just any random coming thing, but that which deactualizes what was hitherto actual. What thus essentially comes toward the human being is the dreamlike aspect of a dreaming that does not lose itself in the indeterminate randomness of the unreal. The dreaming of what is thus dreamlike must look ahead toward the possible in its becoming real and must say this as such in advance, and thus also tell it beforehand (πρόφημι, προφητεύειν).

Plato, in his dialogue concerning the beautiful (the *Phaedrus*), speaks of the μανία προφητεύουσα—of the rapture that tells in advance of that which is not yet fully present. In Hölderlin's late poem "Ripe, bathed in fire . . ." we read (IV, 71):

> Reif sind, in Feuer getaucht, gekochet
> Die Frücht und auf der Erde geprüfet und ein Gesez ist
> Dass alles hineingeht, Schlangen gleich,
> Prophetisch, träumend auf
> Den Hügeln des Himmels.

> Ripe, bathed in fire, cooked
> The fruits and tested on Earth and it is a law
> That everything goes in, like serpents,
> Prophetically, dreaming upon
> The hills of the heavens.

Even if we do not yet understand the slightest thing about these lines, the inner connection between dreaming and the prophetic, between that which is dreamlike and that which is coming, is nevertheless unequivocal. What is thus dreamlike, however, is more real than the commonplace real of everyday use and employment by creatures of the day.

These dreams are therefore called golden, that is, rich, heavy, and replete with "beings" to come, and, because they are coming, illuminating and noble in their radiant glow, that is, essencing within themselves and not requiring what is commonplace.

That which essentially comes and comes toward us can never be reached in a so-called intervention. In the realm of what is essential concerning history, that is, concerning transitions, every "intervention" is a failed intervention, because it destroys what is coming in its coming and drags the possible into something presumedly and contingently actual and real. In the realm of the essential, the human being can never "make" history, no more than can the God. Each of them only ever make their contrivances and their attendant contrivers. To the latter belong in the first instance the intriguers of an ecclesiastical order, because they exploit what is purportedly holy in the service of their own aspirations of power.

The transition accomplishes itself here only in the slowness of hesitant awe in the face of what cannot be made. In the blowing of the breezes heavy with golden dreams, the slow footbridges are the inconspicuous, narrow bridges, originally grown and yet reserved only for a few individuals. These bridges, the footbridges, indeed seem to lack span, since they lead straight and level from one bank to another. Yet their span is not lacking. It is merely concealed to the habitual eye and foot. It is higher than the span of any broad, sweeping bridge can ever be that anyone can hurry over at any time in whatever kind of haste. The height of the footbridges' span is determined in terms of the height and supreme height of the breezes drawing over them, and that is, at the same time, in terms of the gold of the dreams.

The poet's greeting, which is consummated with the end of the second strophe, itself belongs to a transition. The footbridge goes from the end of the second strophe to the beginning of the third strophe.

§43. Greece and Germania: the banks and sides of the transition toward learning what is historically one's own

The transition between strophes indeed seems merely to keep to the externalities of poetic form. In the interim, however, we intimate something of what is poetized in the first two strophes. The southern land and the native homeland of the poet, Greece and Germania, reveal their hidden relation. This relation is not exhausted by relations of a spiritual history of the two "cultures" that can be historiographically narrated. The relation itself grounds itself in the word of a poetic founding. The "fire of the south" and the "barren north" (from the elegy "The Wanderer") do not here designate "types" of lands and peoples that lie present before us, and that can simply be played off against one another in comparative historiographical perspectives. Greece and Germania name the banks and sides of a transition. Because the transition shelters within it the becoming real of the one as the becoming ideal of the other, the transitional telling must also therefore correspond to that which is to be told here. Insofar as the becoming ideal of what was previously actual, and the latter as what once was, must be said in the intimacy of its essence, this telling can only be a greeting.

From where does the poet greet? From his native homeland. Its essence is called "Germania." Here is the other side, to which the poet has already transitioned. Here, everything is different. One's own is something other than that of the Greeks. The foreign, too, is something other; the manner of learning to freely use what is one's own is likewise other. Here, what is most difficult is other, and it can neither be alleviated nor indeed removed through any kind of rebirth of antiquity, through any "Renaissances"; it cannot be found historiographically at all. The essential historical decision in relation to the land of Greece, that is, with regard to its festivals, has been made. The poet has clearly announced it in the hymn "Germania," which was composed three years before "Remembrance." Almost abruptly and free of any concern with escapes or middle courses, decided with respect to need and to bearing the need, the hymn "Germania" begins (IV, 181):

> Nicht sie, die Seeligen, die erschienen sind,
> Die Götterbilder in dem alten Lande,
> Sie darf ich ja nicht rufen mehr, . . .

> Not those, the blessed ones who once appeared,
> Divine images in the land of old,
> Those, indeed, I may call no longer, . . .

The poet presumably still greets those who once have been, but he is no longer permitted to call them, and that means, to await them as those who are to come to the festival and can play a role in determining the festival. Yet by the very fact of the poet's saying that he is no longer permitted to call those who once appeared, who once have been, he indeed says precisely that he is a caller. He speaks out of an awaiting, even if this awaiting is as yet without fulfillment, and indeed even without immediate prospect of any fulfillment, and is more a being deprived, a being abandoned and in need. Yet even if it is plaint and mourning, a joy speaks within it, and from the unity of both, the fundamental attunement for the festival, the awaiting of the festive, and that is, of the holy. The guardian and custodian of the fundamental attunement, the heart, is "the holy mourning one." This is why, at the beginning of the hymn "Germania," the poet continues:

> wenn aber
> Ihr heimatlichen Wasser! jezt mit euch
> Des Herzens Liebe klagt, was will es anders
> Das Heiligtrauernde?

> yet if
> You waters of the homeland! now with you
> The heart's love has plaint, what else does it want,
> The holy mourning one?

What else does it want but to name the holy, yet the holy in its own father-land, in which the poet now remains behind, enduring the northeasterly and the sharpness of its cool clarity? Now he must give up the attempt to seek the gods directly, there where they formerly played a role in determin-ing a day of festival. To want such a thing would, after all, mean to directly retrieve what was inherited by the human beings of the land of Greece as their own, what lay in their cradle, to which they were always returned once more and cradled within it, that by which they were directly attuned through and through. What was their own, and essential to the birthland of the Greeks, is the heavenly fire, glowingly enchanting and delighting as it clears: the radiant gleam of golden dreams. To authentically appropriate this, which was their own, was what was most difficult for the Greeks. What was their own and their manner of appropriating it cannot be that own which "the German poet" must find in his native homeland. This find-ing demands its own seeking, and this seeking, its own learning. A human-kind's freedom in relation to itself consists in finding, appropriating, and being able to use what is one's own. It is in this that the historicality of the history of a people resides. It is not by chance that Hölderlin twice enunci-ates this essential aspect of all history within the same letter to Böhlendorff (December 4, 1801). First as follows (V, 319):

> We learn nothing with greater difficulty than to freely use the national. And as I believe, precisely the clarity of presentation is originally as natural to us, as the fire from the heavens was to the Greeks.

To this hour, we do not yet grasp the truth expressed in the knowledge underlying these sentences. In part, this is due to the fact that we have lit-tle experience of what knowledge means, and expect knowledge to come from "science." This is also why our thinking of history is confused and clueless when faced with the insights that Hölderlin expresses, even if we are familiar with these insights and ponder thoughtfully what is thus famil-iar. Here, we can point out these confused views only to the extent allowed by the task of this interpretation.

For the Greeks, their own is the "fire from the heavens," for the Germans, their own is "the clarity of presentation." Each time, one's own is most readily missed, misconstrued, and lost, because it counts as something self-evident and is therefore either missed, or else taken up in a crude or hasty manner. To find and learn to use one's own is what is most difficult. The fire from the heavens demands appropriation, that is, presentation. The clarity of presentation demands that which is to be presented, the fire from the heavens. One's own does not, therefore, consist in an insulated pre-disposition sealed within itself that could simply be cultivated. Precisely one's own is in each case related to something else, the fire to presentation, presentation to the fire.

One's own cannot be identified by exploring predispositions, as though these were qualities simply cropping up somewhere, relating to nothing or to any random thing. One's own can never be ascertained through cranial measurements or through the description of excavated spears and bracelets, aside from the fact that such results already presuppose what is to count as one's own. Nor are tradition and custom that which is one's own itself; they are rather modes of conduct that have evolved and are a cultivation of one's own that ground themselves in one's own. Such conduct and cultivation can, then, if one's own has already been decided, also be conceived as the "expression" of one's own.

Even the "deeds" of the world are only "signs," and even this only if they are correctly interpreted. Yet how are we to interpret historiographically the immense amount of material that has been historically inherited if we fail to grasp the essence of history to begin with and do not even know the sole domain of reflection within which that essence can and must be asked about? What history is can never be discovered by a historian. Neither the study of folklore [*Volkskunde*], nor geography, nor the discoveries by art history of the so-called German line, nor even historiography find what is one's own; they bring only an accumulation of "manifestations" of that which—no one knows how or from where—they take to be one's own. No science of nature or history ever finds one's own. It never finds it because it is not seeking it, and it is not seeking it because, in accordance with its essence as science, it is not able to seek such a thing. One's own is discovered only by those whose task is to found it, by the poets.

§44. One's own as the holy of the fatherland, inaccessible to theologies and historiographical sciences. The "highest"

We heard already Hölderlin's words from the dedication in his Sophocles translations: "Otherwise . . . if there is time, . . . I want to sing the angels of the holy fatherland." He wants to say the holy, wherein the fatherland has its essence, and those by whom that essence is protected: the angels.

This holy, however, is not simply the divine of some "religion" likewise at hand, here, the Christian one. The holy cannot be ascertained "theologically" at all, for all "theology" already presupposes the Θεός, the god, and this is so emphatically the case that wherever theology arises, the god has already begun his flight.

The Greeks, in the great and authentic period of their history, were without "theology." Neither the theologians of the "German Christians," nor those of the Confessional Front, nor the Catholic theologians can find the holy of the fatherland. They are in the same trap as the biologists, the prehistorians, and the art historians; claiming to be close to reality, they engage in a kind of "intellectualism," one not even attained by the greatly maligned nineteenth century that they blindly continue. One's own is not to be procured so cheaply in an era when the world is threatening to get out of joint. Whoever thinks that it can be, is denigrating the concealed dignity of the ownmost essence of the fatherland, and, if he is thinking at all, is in any case not thinking in a German manner.

This confusion in knowing and in being able to know first attains its pinnacle, however, where one is of the view that the rejection of these mistaken intentions—namely, to want to ascertain the essential scientifically, that is, today always in a rational-organizational-technical manner—that this rejection is equivalent to the denial of one's own and of what is German. The opposite is true. With this, however, we must also ponder the fact that rejecting the "rational" may not be equated with the equally cheap appeal to the "irrational"; for the latter is only the milk brother of the "rational" and is groundless in the same way as the "rational," and, moreover, is in every case still dependent on how the "rational" that is being negated has been determined beforehand.

Yet if the poet is to find his own and the holy of the fatherland, then he is not allowed to appeal to a resourcefulness or cunning that he himself has contrived, or to any kind of astuteness. The historical, that is, festive essence of his own fatherland is something that the poet must *seek*. Already in the first fragment of *Hyperion* we find Hölderlin's obscure word (II, 81): "We are nothing; what we seek is everything." Yet this early word then changes its meaning, even though the "holy mourning heart," the seeking, remains the fundamental attunement of the poet.

Only in seeking is that which is sought close to us. What is being sought is the enchanting figure of what is found by the seeking. Only in that which is sought does what is found come to shine. Where that which is found has become a mere find, it is already fit for the museum and donated to the museum and thus lost—an object for Americans. (The surrender of the German essence to Americanism, to its own detriment, on occasion goes so far that Germans are ashamed of the fact that their people was once called "the people of poets and thinkers.")

Poetizing and thinking is authentic seeking. Such seeking is questioning. The poet is not able to ascertain the holy like a bone; he must question the holy itself. This means: the poet must ask the one who has safeguarded for him that which is to be said, the holy: the Muse. The mother of the Muses is Mnemosyne, in German: *Andenken*, remembrance. From Hölderlin's hymnal period one fragment has been preserved that says everything. The fragment reads (IV, 249):

> Einst hab ich die Muse gefragt, und sie
> Antwortete mir
> Am Ende wirst du es finden.
> Vom Höchsten will ich schweigen.
> Verbotene Frucht, wie der Lorbeer, ist aber
> Am meisten das Vaterland. Die aber kost'
> Ein jeder zulezt.

> Once I asked the Muse, and she
> Answered me
> In the end you will find it.
> Concerning what is highest, I will be silent.
> Forbidden fruit, like the laurel, is, however,
> Above all the fatherland. Such, however, each
> Shall taste last.

What is ownmost, the fatherland, is the highest, yet for that reason, it is what is most forbidden. This is why it is found only at the end, after long searching, after many sacrifices and hard service. Each may taste this fruit only last, only when each is prepared, when nothing forced continues to dissemble a free view of the highest, when nothing importunate confuses or scares off that which is forbidden. That which belongs to the fatherland will be found only when the highest is sought. To seek the highest means to be silent concerning it. Yet this keeping silent does not pass over the highest but rather preserves it. This preserving is necessary, for only from the highest can we attain what is high. We never reach what is high from below, only ever from above.

Yet how is it with keeping silent that which is highest? Only someone who, from time to time, truly says something can truly keep silent. Mere not saying is not yet a keeping silent. For the sake of this keeping silent, the word must, therefore, be taken up and said. For only he who says what is right can, in such saying, keep silent what is highest. This saying, however, and it first and foremost, must be found beforehand. The free use of one's own word concerning one's own is what is most difficult. What is one's own and native, the Earth of the homeland, the Mother, is most difficult to attain. This is why Hölderlin, entirely in keeping with the sense of the letter to his friend, says in the hymn "The Journey" (IV, 170):

Unfreundlich ist, und schwer zu gewinnen,
Die Verschlossene, der ich entkommen, die Mutter.

Unfriendly, and difficult to attain, is
The Closed One from which I have come, the Mother.

Do we now intimate the difficulty that lies in the fact that the poet remains behind in his native homeland? Are we able to fathom the kind of waiting from which the greeting stems of that land in which the poet is no longer allowed to remain? Can we thoughtfully ponder how someone must be, in order to be able to truly greet, and to greet in the manner that the poet does in the first two strophes of "Remembrance"? Do we intimate what this means: to remain behind in the homeland and to seek here one's own? Do we have the slightest intimation of the forbearance [*Langmut*] belonging to seeking thus in the homeland? Yet do we also intimate the magnanimity [*Großmut*] that must be proper to such forbearance, so that each who seeks his own and the fatherland can bring more freely into a free realm the free use of his own? Are we now still surprised when Hölderlin himself, in the poem "Ripe, bathed in fire . . ." composed shortly after "Remembrance" (in 1805), says the following (IV, 71):

. . . . Und vieles
Wie auf den Schultern eine
Last von Scheitern ist
Zu behalten.

. . . . And much
As on one's shoulders a
Burden of logs is
To be retained.

Are we surprised when the poet who knows in this manner asked the Muse, and also understood her in what she herself wants and what, in keeping with this will, she demands of the poet: that he must keep silent concerning the highest? To keep silent here means to say all that is to be said, in such a way that it is intimated as that which is kept silent and, as something intimated, becomes that which pervasively attunes and determines all the long-waiting seeking. Where is this keeping silent in the poem "Remembrance"? In the transition from the second strophe, in whose conclusion the greeting of the other land and festival is consummated, to the third strophe. Between the two is an abyss; steeply dropping and towering like cliffs stand the conclusion of the second strophe, which indeed also embraces the first, and the beginning of the third.

In this abyss lies the keeping silent of that which is to be kept silent and is kept silent.

§45. The transition from the second to the third strophe. Grounding in the homely

The transition from the second to the third strophe goes over a footbridge and contains a decision. The third strophe reads:

> Es reiche aber,
> Des dunkeln Lichtes voll,
> Mir einer den duftenden Becher,
> Damit ich ruhen möge; denn süß
> Wär' unter Schatten der Schlummer.
> Nicht ist es gut
> Seellos von sterblichen
> Gedanken zu seyn. Doch gut
> Ist ein Gespräch und zu sagen
> Des Herzens Meinung, zu hören viel
> Von Tagen der Lieb',
> Und Thaten, welche geschehen.

> Yet may someone reach me,
> Full of dark light,
> The fragrant cup,
> That I may rest; for sweet
> Would be the slumber among shadows.
> It is not good
> To be soulless of mortal
> Thoughts. But good
> Is a dialogue and to say
> The heart's opinion, to hear much
> Of days of love,
> And deeds that occur.

This strophe begins abruptly and disconcertingly, like a capricious leaping over from one idea and image to another. Yet the transition to this strophe becomes clearer to us if we keep in mind what was noted thus far and now, perhaps in a somewhat schematic and forced manner, ponder the first three strophes simply in terms of those lines in which the poet tells of himself, the poet, and expresses his essence.

In the first strophe we find:

> Geh aber nun und grüsse

> But go now and greet

The poet, in greeting, remains behind in his own land. Yet this remaining behind does not repel that which is greeted. The land of Greece is not forgotten, nor denied, but retained. Thus we may complete the line by saying, "But go now and greet [for me]." Accordingly, the second strophe also begins:

> Noch denket das mir wohl . . .

> Still it thinks its way to me . . .

The one who remains behind is himself remembered together with that which he greets, that is, a gift is bestowed upon him in a peculiar way. The one who greets experiences himself being greeted. The festival that once was recalls the intimate, which as the holy is that which properly greets. That which properly greets beckons the one who remains behind to call upon the holy of the fatherland from his locale and to be at home within the protection of this, the highest. Remaining behind in his own, yet still unappropriated fatherland does not, therefore, happen against his will, but out of the assent on the part of the greeting poet to that which, in greeting, calls upon him to find what is his own. The poet is neither cut off from what once was, nor left alone in some empty cluelessness. He belongs to that which once was, yet does so from the difficulty of preparing for what is most difficult: to learn the free use of his own, so that in such freedom the free and open realm may form itself in which the holy of his fatherland can appear. Yet because the poet is delivered over to this most difficult task, he must renounce taking immediate refuge in what once was, or merely adopting what once was as passed down. This renouncing is a deprivation and need, yet one that nevertheless does not spring from a mere lack but from his assenting to appropriate what is his own.

In the third strophe we read:

> Es reiche aber,
> . . . .
> Mir einer den duftenden Becher,

> Yet may someone reach me,
> . . . .
> The fragrant cup,

The pure granting of the lulling breezes is followed in sharp contrast by the call for something that is first to be reached. The *aber* ["yet"] in "Es reiche aber" ["Yet may (someone) reach"] only sharpens the contrast, which at first remains in a peculiar indeterminacy by virtue of the *Es* ["It"] at the start of the line. This peculiar indeterminacy is by no means removed by the *einer* ["someone"] in the third line of the strophe. The call that arises, as though out of nothing, for a bringing and bestowing, as though greeting and what is greeted had suddenly been swallowed up, has not yet been adequately interpreted with what has been noted. If we allow the lines we have extracted from the first three strophes to directly follow one another:

> Geh aber nun und grüsse [mir]
> _____
>
> Noch denket das mir wohl . . .
> _____
>
> Es reiche aber,
> . . . .
> Mir . . .
>
> But go now and greet [for me]
> _____
>
> Still it thinks its way to me . . .
> _____
>
> Yet may someone reach me,
> . . . .
> The . . .

Then we indeed recognize the abyss between the act of greeting and the call of need, yet we now also are in danger once again of indeed still misinterpreting the essential connections. Thus, it may seem as though the word of need, "Yet may someone reach . . ." is only the consequence of the fact that what is greeted henceforth remains something foreign and something that once was and has nothing more to bestow, so that the greeting too appears almost like an erroneous lapse. In truth, however, everything is already otherwise. The act of greeting springs already, and springs only, from the return to finding one's own, a return that has already been decided and undertaken. What is their own for the Germans is the clarity of presentation. What is their own for the Greeks is the fire from the heavens—the golden dreams. In *Hyperion*, the young Greek writes to his friend (II, 92):

> Oh, the human being is a god when he dreams,
> a beggar when he thinks . . .

The poem "Remembrance" begins: "The northeasterly blows, / Most beloved of the winds / To me." Now that we know that in "Remembrance" the historicity of the history of the fatherland is being thought, the opening line first unveils its full truth. The wind, which makes the eyes steadfast, guarantees the clear boldness of our looking (setting before us and presenting). The wind in the native homeland is a promise for what is given the poet as his most difficult task. The northeasterly is the most beloved not only because it is suited to carry the greeting off to southern France. It can do that too; it is meant to do this also precisely because the poet is intimately familiar with it as the wind of his native homeland. "The northeasterly blows"—this now says: the task is to hold out in the ether and element of clarity, and to find therein the law of one's own. It is because the poet has returned to his own and to seeking his own, and is decided, that he is first able to acknowledge the foreign in its essence, from out of such acknowledgment to recognize it in what is its own, and therefore to greet that which thus essentially prevails within itself as what once was. That which once was, the foreign, by contrast, is preserved from out of one's own and for one's own. One's own "is" first proper and authentic only in being appropriated. This, however, cannot happen without the dialogue with the foreign. The land of Greece is not only not thrust away; it has in a new sense become historically necessary.

With this remark, a further misinterpretation of Hölderlin's poetizing, one that has already become prevalent today, now becomes untenable.

§46. Interim remark concerning three misinterpretations of Hölderlin's turn to the "fatherland"

It has been known, especially since von Hellingrath's publication of the hymns, that after 1800 Hölderlin underwent a turn that became clearer from one year to the next, a turn that goes together with a new relationship to the Greek world. And because the fatherland, the German, is sought in this turn, people have spoken of a "turn to the land of evening" on the part of Hölderlin, and in this conceived of the Greek world as the "land of morning," and of the relationship to it even as a turning away.[14] Yet this was only the prelude for a further intention.

The turn to the land of evening came to be interpreted as a turn toward Christendom. In the period of his hymns, Hölderlin indeed speaks of "Christ" and of the "Madonna." Yet any careful thought will recognize that this Christian turn of Hölderlin's that is proclaimed for various reasons is an invention.

By contrast, another turn seems to be clearer and less equivocal: the turn to the fatherland. What is more obvious than to interpret the turn to the fatherland along the lines of a turn to the "political"? However, what Hölderlin names the fatherland is not exhausted by the "political," no matter how broadly one may conceive the latter.

All three views are erroneous. The new relationship to the Greek world is not a turn away but a more essential turn toward the Greek world, one that presses in the direction of a more original confrontation with it, yet indeed without seeking in it the origin and ground of one's own. The turn to the fatherland is not a flight to Christendom; to the extent that Christ is spoken of, he is only one among the gods, a way of thinking that cannot in truth be called "Christian." The turn to the fatherland is not the turn to the political either, however.

Even if one were able to equate the fatherland and the political, we would have to ponder the fact that the fatherland is a fruit that can grow only in the light and ether, in the element of the highest, that is, of the holy. The holy is the ground of the fatherland and of its historical essence. The fatherland is the highest only when, and insofar as, it stems from the highest, from the holy, and this, its ownmost origin, has been found as what is authentically its own, so that each at last shall have his portion of this, which is first. Learning to freely use one's own is most difficult, for free use alone is the correct manner of preserving one's own, and is even the sole way of first finding one's own. This alone sheds light on why the poet around this period, when he has, after all, come home, nevertheless speaks of the heavy burden and lets us know that much still remains to be said.

If the turn to the holy of the fatherland were only a taking refuge in the safe haven of Christian belief or an immersion in the present domain of political activity, then it would not be discernible why these refuges and these immediately satisfying occupations should be a burden and a need that must first be long withstood, given that, to the contrary, they guarantee the security of the soul's salvation and the satisfaction of direct action and success. Yet in this poetizing there is nothing of security or satisfaction anywhere—everything is a task. This poetizing is not a standpoint but a passage, the passage of learning to appropriate one's own.

§47. Learning the appropriation of one's own

> Es reiche aber,
> Des dunkeln Lichtes voll,
> Mir einer den duftenden Becher,
> Damit ich ruhen möge;

Yet may someone reach me,
Full of dark light,
The fragrant cup,
That I may rest;

Yet does this sound like setting out on the path to one's own? Is this how
the boldness of attaining one's own speaks? Is this not, rather, a weary call
for help, so as to be able to avoid the passage to one's own, to withdraw
from one's own and the foreign at the same time, and to be no longer
disturbed by anything? Does not Hölderlin say this clearly enough: "That
I may rest"? He seeks rest, thus a pause in his path, thus the casting off
of his burden, thus surely the opposite of what, according to our previous
discussions, is supposed to start with the third strophe.

Yet we would do well to keep in mind the whole of the first part of the
third strophe, over and beyond a few words taken out of context. The first
part closes only with the words:

denn süß
Wär' unter Schatten der Schlummer.

for sweet
Would be the slumber among shadows.

It does not read: for sweet "is" the slumber among shadows. Such slumber
"would" be sweet only if things were allowed to come to that, which is to
say, if rest were here synonymous with sleeping. It indeed appears to be
better to sleep and thus to glide off into oblivion. However, this is not the
vocation of the poet, and therefore also, if he is indeed to rest, not the manner in which he rests amid shadows and in the night. He must indeed be a
wanderer "in holy night," but for him this means: remaining awake for the
holy, which the night prepares for and encloses within it. Let us ponder in
this regard the seventh strophe of the elegy "Bread and Wine." It concludes
with a word concerning the poets who are now being called (IV, 124):

Aber sie sind, sagst du, wie des Weingotts heilige Priester,
Welche von Lande zu Land zogen in heiliger Nacht.

Yet they are, you say, like the wine god's holy priests,
Who journeyed from land to land in holy night.

Twice the holy is named. The poets, however, who now wander through
the night as the time-space of the gods that once were and have fled, are

brought into a relation to the god of wine, to Bacchus, Dionysus. For this reason, in the manner of the usual historiographical comparing and reckoning together, people have thrown Hölderlin's distinction between what belongs to the Greeks and to the Germans as their own together with Nietzsche's distinction between the Dionysian and the Apollonian. One sticks to the mere words that sound the same and fails to consider thoughtfully what the words say. Thus in one book that is widely read today we encounter the horrendous representation of Hölderlin as the "Swabian Nietzsche." The distinction made by Nietzsche and its role in his metaphysics of the will to power is not Greek but rather rooted in the metaphysics of modernity. Hölderlin's distinction, by contrast, we must learn to understand as the harbinger of the overcoming of all metaphysics.

The god of wine is a god that once was. There is no "Dionysian in itself." Presumably, by contrast, wine retains an essential role in determining the future festival and for its preparation by the poet:

> Es reiche aber,
> Des dunkeln Lichtes voll,
> Mir einer den . . . Becher,
> . . . . . .

> Yet may someone reach me,
> Full of dark light,
> The . . . cup,
> . . . . . .

If wine is being named here, then these words do not call for an opportunity to avoid the passage toward appropriating one's own. To the contrary, the celebration is to be prepared. Preparation here means "learning the free use of one's own"; it means holding out in what is most difficult. What is one's own for the land in which the poet now comes to be at home? It has already been named several times now according to the word of the letter to Böhlendorff: "the clarity of presentation."

§48. What is their own for the Germans: "the clarity of presentation"

Yet what does this mean: "the clarity of presentation"? We know on the basis of the treatise on the "fatherland in decline" that "presentation" is essential in "dissolution" and "becoming." If the "clarity of presentation" is natural and proper to the Germans, then precisely this, which is their own, remains at first that which is least of all appropriated. Indeed, it can be that "in the progress of cultivation," precisely one's own is increasingly lost, because its free use has not been learned. "Progress" of cultivation is the further cultivation of a present at hand predisposition that has precisely been identified, the fulfilling of tendencies announcing themselves within it, the achievement of whatever these strive for, securing the capacity to achieve them, cultivating the predisposition into a characteristic that is securely controlled.

This use of one's own, however, which merely exercises and uses one's own as a predisposition at hand, is not its free use, for here a human-kind remains constricted into its predisposition that is simply ascertained and taken up at some point and in some way. The humankind in this way remains the blind servant of a predisposition that is blindly seized upon. How so blind and blindly? Because what is not seen here and cannot be seen here is what first makes every predisposition and characteristic into such—that for which it is a predisposition, or expressed more clearly: that which is to be presented in clear presentation. This does not at all emerge from the mere ability for clear presentation—to the contrary, this ability can bring itself to decide from out of itself what it is that has been pre-sented and is to be presented, and how it is to be presented. The use of one's own in this manner reflects only on how to exercise the predisposi-tion, which is restricted to itself and its being contingently at hand. The use is then merely self-serving; it is not free, and it is also not the free use of one's own because how one's own is determined springs in part from that for which it is determined and by which it is attuned.

For the use of one's own to become a free use, one's own must be open for that which is assigned it. The clarity of presentation will never find its way to itself, so long as it merely exercises itself as an empty ability within the indeterminate and arbitrary. What is needed is for one's own here, the clarity of presentation, to let itself be determined by what such presentation demands. The clarity enters a free realm only when it meas-ures itself, tests and fulfills itself, according to the dark, and thus first becomes mature. The free does not consist in the unhindered arbitrariness of something groundless. Freedom is openness toward what is originary and inceptual. Learning the free use of one's own, this task that is the most difficult, means learning to open oneself for what is originary, which by contrast with all self-centeredness is that which is other and other in prove-nance, almost in the manner of something altogether foreign. This learning to open oneself for what is assigned, in whose presentation one's own first attains freedom, must therefore begin with a readiness for that wherein alone, as in the other, the clarity of presentation can be tested. And what is

this: the dark of that which has not yet been presented, that which awaits
presentation and being cultivated:

> Es reiche aber,
> Des dunkeln Lichtes voll,
> Mir einer den . . . Becher,
> . . . . . .

> Yet may someone reach me,
> Full of dark light,
> The . . . cup,
> . . . . . .

However, a reservation announces itself once again.

§49. The drunkenness of higher reflection and soberness of presentation in the word

Learning to use freely the clarity of presentation: does that not, before all
else, mean becoming sober? However, does the request "may someone
reach" not want instead the numbing and forgetting and intoxicated rapture of one who fails to reflect? Surely, learning the free use of clear presentation by contrast demands before all else self-reflection. Certainly. Yet
what does it mean to reflect here? Surely not mere reckoning, calculating
how something is to be arranged and contrived from the circumstances?
Reflecting must be concerned with something else, with that which is to be
presented and which determines the manner of presentation.

What is to be presented is history, becoming in dissolution, the coming
of the festival. The festival is the history of the holy. The holy, however, is
the highest. For this reason, reflection must be of a higher kind and stem
from a thinking whose origin is itself in keeping with the holy that is to
come into the word and to presentation. Hölderlin knows of this necessity
of such higher reflection and of its origin. In the unfinished elegy "The
Walk in the Country" (IV, 112, lines 13ff.), Hölderlin says:

> Darum hoff ich sogar, es werde, wenn das Gewünschte
> Wir beginnen, und erst unsere Zunge gelöst,
> Und gefunden das Wort, und aufgegangen das Herz ist,
> Und von trunkener Stirn' höher Besinnen entspringt,
> Mit der unsern zugleich des Himmels Blüthe beginnen,
> Und dem offenen Blik offen der Leuchtende seyn.

Thus I even hope that when we begin
What is wished for, and once our tongues are loosened,
And the word found, and our heart has arisen,
And from drunken brow springs higher reflection,
The heaven's blossom shall begin together with ours,
And open to the open look be the one illuminating.

Higher reflection springs "from drunken brow." Thus rapture and intoxication are indeed required. Whence, therefore, the request to pass the full cup of wine; thus the demand, after all, for a means of excitation and stimulation. Yet we would go far astray, were we to think in this way.

In the first place, is drunkenness merely intoxication? To begin with, intoxication and intoxication are not always the same thing. Intoxication as mere inebriation is different from the intoxication of enthusiasm. Drunkenness is something different again from both of these. It means a being fulfilled that is neither merely blind frenzy nor unreflective transport. Drunkenness means a being fulfilled that entails a unique gathering and readiness. Drunkenness is that sublimity of attunement that is resolved to the most extreme other of itself; resolved not by virtue of some calculated decision, but resolved, presumably, on the basis of a being borne by that which thoroughly pervades it as an attunement. The "drunken brow" does not confuse and fog our thinking; rather, the sustained sublimity of the attunement transposes it into the height from which reflection can be of a higher kind. It thus remains in proximity to the highest, which Hölderlin names the holy. The request for "the fragrant cup," "full of dark light," is not a demand for numbing and intoxication, but for the attunement of the higher reflecting that thinks the holy and is sober as thinking.

This soberness, admittedly, is different from our habitual soberness, which in turn can be of two kinds. There is the sober aspect of that which is unassuming and yet sound and certain of itself. This soberness, as *one* figure of the simple, does not need to be a shortcoming, unlike that other "soberness" that first presents itself in what is sparse and empty, dry and listless.

The soberness of higher thinking is different. To it there belongs the boldness of tarrying in the heights of the highest. This soberness is also by no means a sobering up from drunkenness, as though the latter were to be kept in check or even eliminated. This soberness is filled with drunkenness, and the latter finds in the former that which corresponds to it, addresses it and raises it into the word, that is, presents it.

From the sphere of the poem "Remembrance," and published by Hölderlin himself at the same time as that poem, comes the poem entitled "Midpoint of Life." This poem, too, may in no way be interpreted as "lyrical." Its truth, deeply veiled in the most beautiful images, stands in an essential relation to the hymnal poetizing and to the transition into the homely and its grounding that is undertaken in that poetizing. The first of the poem's two strophes reads (IV, 60):

> Mit gelben Birnen hänget
> Und voll mit wilden Rosen
> Das Land in den See,
> Ihr holden Schwäne,
> Und trunken von Küssen
> Tunkt ihr das Haupt
> Ins heilignüchterne Wasser.

> With yellow pears hangs down
> And full of wild roses,
> The land into the lake,
> You beloved swans,
> And drunken with kisses
> You dip your crowns
> Into the holy-sober water.

The very fact that we are told of the "crowns" of the swans by itself leaves us astonished. The crown is not simply the head; "the crown" recalls the nobility of the brow and the origin of thinking. Yet the brow, too, is here not meant anatomically as the skull bone. How the word is meant, we can scarcely say in the right manner, and yet we know it, as soon as we do not dissect the human form "biologically," something we still continue to do when we make a hollow sound with the vacuous din of expressions such as "wholeness" and the like.

The crown, the brow, higher reflection have their element in the "holy-sober water." Dipping into this is not cooling off as relief and overcoming of drunkenness, but the unfolding of drunkenness in the element of the clear.

§50. "Dark light": that which is to be presented in the free use of one's own

> Es reiche aber,
> Des dunkeln Lichtes voll,
> Mir einer den duftenden Becher,
> . . . . . .

> Yet may someone reach me,
> Full of dark light,

The fragrant cup,

. . . . . .

This is the call for that which must first be brought to and bestowed upon the ability of clear presentation as that which is to be presented, into whose darkness and hiddenness presentation fits itself, so that it may achieve clarity by way of such correspondence. Now we intimate for the first time why Hölderlin uses for wine that word whose beauty is so uncanny, because it says everything in supreme simplicity.

For our habitual thinking, something like "the dark light" is a blatant contradiction, and therefore the sign of impossibility. A light, if only the faintest, is surely always bright, or at least such that it wards off darkness. Here, by contrast, is an illumination that comes to shine through its darkness, so that here something appears in concealing itself. It refuses manifestness and thus raises presentation into the boldness, not of replacing the dark illumination by an empty brightness, but rather of corresponding to it in the clarity of presentation to be attained. Through such correspondence, presentation enters the free realm of its essence, if freedom indeed consists in letting oneself be originarily and solely determined by what is originary.

The word of the "dark light," of which the fragrant cup is full, by no means contains only a particularly felicitous, poetical image for the wine, but rather names that which is to be presented, to which the clarity of presentation must fit itself in advance if it is to be capable of learning the free use of itself. Here, learning to freely use one's own is learning to unfold the excellence of the gift of presentation, and doing so out of a relationship to that which must be presented and is not one's own that has been imported, but the foreign.

Yet this foreign, too, and the relationship to it, must be learned, and this together with one's own. For the foreign, and thereby that which is to be offered, can be unfittingly received, so that instead of awakening the appropriation of one's own, it lets it be forgotten.

§51. The danger of slumber among shadows. "Soulful" reflection upon the holy in the festival

The dark light being offered in the fragrant cup can thus indeed lead astray into tasting the sweetness of slumber in mere unrestrained enjoyment, thus avoiding the light and seeking the security of the shade:

denn süss
Wär' unter Schatten der Schlummer.

> for sweet
> Would be the slumber among shadows.

However, the poet who has traversed the footbridge and thus come home is decided in his knowledge of that which alone can be the highest for him; certainly, he also knows, as the letter to Böhlendorff says that deals with the learning of one's own and the foreign, "that it is godless and crazy to seek a path that would be secure from *all* attack . . ." (V, 321). Yet the same resolve that in the poem calls "May someone reach . . .," when faced with the danger of becoming submerged in what is offered gives the clear announcement:

> Nicht ist es gut
> Seellos von sterblichen
> Gedanken zu seyn.

> It is not good
> To be soulless
> Of mortal thoughts.

Like a sharp cut, the holy resolve to learn one's own intervenes between the concluding word of the previous lines, which speak of sweet slumber, and that which follows. "It is not good . . ."—even the favored "But" that might suggest itself here is lacking; this "not . . ." follows abruptly and disconnected.

Simply to become submerged in the sweetness of slumber under the protection of shade would mean "to be soulless of mortal thoughts." What does this mean: "mortal thoughts"? That "thoughts" are transitory; that transitoriness affects precisely "thoughts," which anyhow as "mere thoughts" remain already unreal and without subsistence, as distinct from what is real and effective in our endeavors and action?

"Mortal thoughts" here means those thoughts that are proper to mortals. The mortals are the human beings, and Hölderlin uses this word for the human essence precisely when he contrasts the sons of the Earth and human beings to the gods, that is, when he is thinking of the encountering of humans and gods. This encountering, however, transpires as the event of the festival. "Human thinking" is here not simply thinking carried out by humans but that thinking which constitutes the ground of the human essence and attunes it to its vocation. This thinking is that reflecting which reflects upon the holy that happens in the event of the festival. Thinking in terms of the holiday opens itself to the holy; to think thus is the calling of those whose word names the holy. This is why "now," after the transition has occurred, there is "A fire ignited in the souls of the poets" ("As when on a holiday . . ."). Without that thinking which thinks "humanly" in the direction of what is essential in the human, the poet would be "soulless"— he would be without "soul" and therefore would also be unable to be "the besouler." What do "soul" and "besouling," and accordingly the "soulless," signify here? Words and concepts like "soul," "spirit," "thoughts," "think- ing" have long since become ambiguous for us by virtue of a complex tradition and have therefore become confused and thus given over to arbi- trary usage.

In such situations we like to take refuge in historiographical overviews. A catalog of the various stages in the history of the concept of soul can indeed instruct us about many things. Yet from such instruction we learn nothing, unless we open ourselves to reflection. We ourselves, we of today, must gain a relationship to what Hölderlin means when he says "soul."

This demand for a vital appreciation of what pertains to the soul has indeed been accommodated for several decades by the metaphysics of Nietzsche and the manner in which it is interpreted. One restores priority to the soul over the spirit. In this, it is taken for granted, of course, that the traditional tripartite division of body, soul, and spirit names the compon- ents from which the human essence is constructed. "Soul" is then con- ceived, in a certain borrowing of Aristotle's thought, as the "principle" of life; the soul besouls, or animates, the body. The soul is essential because it animates the body, and because the body, as it bodies forth and lives, is for Nietzsche identified as the guiding thread for interpreting the world in general. In a note from the year 1885, Nietzsche says: "Essential: proceed from the *body* and use it as the guiding thread. It is the far richer phenom- enon, which admits of clearer observation. Belief in the body is better established than belief in the spirit."[1]

In the first part of *Thus Spoke Zarathustra*, in the section "Of the Despis- ers of the Body," Nietzsche says: "But the awakened one, the knower, says: I am body through and through, and nothing besides; and soul is just a word for something about the body." In Nietzsche's sense, "animation," or "besouling," means permeating and liberating the body in its impulses and drives. What pertains to the "soul" as that which bodies forth in the body has priority over the "spirit," which one equates with the "intellect." What pertains to the soul has priority, not because the soul is meant in the Christian sense and thought as "immortal" by contrast with the transitori- ness of the body, but the reverse: because the impulsive driving of the body is regarded as "the eternal" and "soul" is the name for that which drives in this driving, for that which is active in its activity. Spirit, understood as

---

1 *The Will to Power, §532.*

"intellect," by contrast inhibits and weakens the drives, and is therefore branded as "the adversary of the soul."[2] Insofar as these views and this talk about spirit and soul remains vague, it even seems clear to everyone that this order of ranking soul and spirit has hit upon what is "correct"; for who does not know that a human being can be very "full of spirit" and yet "soulless."

However, does soul here mean so straightforwardly the same thing as in the aforementioned interpretation? No—soul now means what we also call the *Gemüt*.[15] Admittedly, this name has lost the authentic force of its naming for us. We need only trace the directions of meaning discernible in the words *gemütlich* [comfortable, cozy], *gemütvoll* [sentimental], *gemüts-krank* [emotionally disturbed]. The *Gemüt* is, then, something tender, if not indeed susceptible and yielding; in any case, something sensitive, "sentimental," "unheroic." However, the word *Gemüt* has yet another, hidden resonance that we shall one day hear once more: *Gemut*, the source and site of *muot*—of *Mut* [cheer, courage] in the original sense that *Mut* is the origin and intimacy of *Gleichmut* [equanimity] and *Armut* [poverty], of *Sanftmut* [gentleness] and *Edelmut* [generosity], of *Anmut* [gracefulness] and *Opfer-mut* [self-sacrifice], of *Großmut* [magnanimity] and *Langmut* [forbearance]. The *Gemüt*, experienced in this way, and "thought" neither psychologically nor biologically, is what Hölderlin names with the word "soul."

Thoughts and thinking do not let the human being be "soulless," yet nor do they first equip him with a "soul," but rather bestow to him the inner-most awakening and releasing of the *Gemüt* to that high *Mut* [cheer]. The opposite of "soulless" is not simply the "possession of soul," but the "soul-ful," the *Hochgemute* [cheerfulness], the *Mut* [cheer] for what is highest.

In the letter to Böhlendorff that we have now mentioned often, Hölderlin, in connection with the discussion concerning the appropriation of one's own and the foreign, says of Homer that "this extraordinary human being was soulful enough to capture Occidental, *Junonian sobriety* for his Apollo-nian kingdom, and thus to truly appropriate the foreign" (V, 319). "Apollo" is for Hölderlin the name for what is light and fiery and glowing—for that which Nietzsche thinks as the Dionysian and contrasts with the Apollonian.

Spirit, in the thinking of its thoughts, is neither "the adversary of the soul" nor the soul's mere servant:

> Nicht ist es gut
> Seellos von sterblichen
> Gedanken zu seyn.

---

2 Ludwig Klages, *Der Geist als Widersacher der Seele* [*Spirit as Adversary of the Soul*], vols. 1–3 (Leipzig, 1929–1933); second improved edition, vols. 1–2 (Leipzig, 1937–1939).

> It is not good
> To be soulless
> Of mortal thoughts.

Thoughts are the thinking of spirit. Spirit is the consummation, which is to say, the originary fulfillment and fullness of the soul. From out of spirit, the human being is first "soulful." In inspiration prevails the original *Mut* of the *Gemüt*. To be without that which pervasively attunes the *Gemüt* and grants the full "essence" of the soul, to be without thinking in accordance with the manner of mortals, that is not good.

> Nicht ist es gut

> It is not good

This is said outright, as though a "sentence," a general "wisdom of life" and rule were to be expressed. However, this "It is not good" is spoken here in the poem by the poet to the poet, and indeed to that poet who has accomplished the transition to the homely and who must now preserve the peace in which there is borne, in a gathered manner, that which is to prepare itself with the offering of the dark light. Such are the holidays of Germania, the days before its festival. The task is to wait out in the German night watches for destiny. This is why, before all else, that which is fitting is demanded in preparation for the festival, that which fittingly sends itself into what is essential in the coming history. "It is not good"—here, "good" means nothing other than "fitting," namely, fitting for the singular and inceptual moment of the other arrival of the gods. That is the while of the equalization of destiny.

Part Four

The Dialogue with the Friends as Fitting Preparation for the Festival

§52. *"Dialogue" in the commonplace understanding and in Hölderlin's poetic word usage*

The task is to seek what is fitting for one's destiny. Only what is fitting gives the suitability proper to one's own. Only from out of one's own, and directed toward it, can the human being truly receive what is coming. What, now, is that which is fitting in this sense? What is fitting, if unfitting is the absence of essentially human thinking in the poet's waiting? What is good, if it is not good to neglect thinking and pondering thoughtfully that wherein the authentic being at home of mortals resides?

> Doch gut
> Ist ein Gespräch und zu sagen
> Des Herzens Meinung, zu hören viel
> Von Tagen der Lieb',
> Und Thaten, welche geschehen.

> Yet good
> Is a dialogue and to say
> The heart's opinion, to hear much
> Of days of love,
> And deeds that occur.

Good is "a dialogue." What a "dialogue" is, we appear to know: individual and multiple human beings talking with one another. However, even in our everyday understanding, we place a certain emphasis on the word "dialogue." Not every instance of talking with one another is already a dialogue. Dialogue counts for us as a particular kind of talking with one another. Sometimes we use it to refer to what we also call a "discussion," in which a "matter" or a "case" is mutually clarified and brought into the clear. Sometimes "dialogue" signifies the bringing about of an encounter: "to enter into dialogue with one another"; this means: to assume relations, to negotiate. Even though in these cases already we always mean by the word dialogue a distinctive kind of talking with one another, nevertheless the equating of dialogue and discussion, dialogue and negotiation, dialogue and communication does not yet hit upon what Hölderlin names poetically with this word.

From the very intricate and far-reaching draft of a hymn that begins "Conciliator, you who never believed . . ." we know that "the dialogue" is the name for the encountering of humans and gods;[3] this not in general, however, but rather for that coming festival that will be "on the evening of time." "Dialogue" here does not refer to the mere form in which language is enacted. In keeping with its original essence, the dialogue is that which unites in the encountering, that through which humans and gods address their essence to one another. The dialogue, regarded in this way, is the "heavenly dialogue."

Yet because for humans *and* for gods their essence is in each case the need of their essence, they admit to one another their essence in the dialogue. Such admittance is the sustaining ground for mutual understanding, that is, the possibility of listening to one another and of hearing from one another. The dialogue is festive in essence.

The dialogue, regarded in this way, is not a form of the use of language. Rather, language has its origin in the dialogue, and that means, in the festival, and thereby in that in which the festival itself is grounded. What a language is and whether the words of a language still speak within the realm of the essence of the word on a given occasion can never be discovered by a "grammar book" or decided by any linguistic science.

§53. The "opinion" of the "heart" in the dialogue: the holy

The meaning that the word "dialogue" fulfills in the poem "Remembrance" also belongs in the circle of the inceptual essence of language. It is a "festive" meaning, essentially related to the festival. How "dialogue" is to be clarified here, Hölderlin tells us himself:

> Doch gut
> Ist ein Gespräch und zu sagen
> . . . . zu hören . . .

> Yet good
> Is a dialogue and to say
> . . . . to hear . . .

---

3 Cf. "Hölderlin und das Wesen der Dichtung," 1936, in *Erläuterungen zu Hölderlins Dichtung*, fourth edition (Frankfurt am Main, 1971), 33–48. Translated by Keith Hoeller as "Hölderlin and the Essence of Poetry," in *Elucidations of Hölderlin's Poetry* (Amherst, NY: Humanity Books, 2000), 51–65. Gesamtausgabe Band 4 (Frankfurt: Klostermann, 1981), 79–151.

The "and" does not add something further, but elucidates: "and" here means so much as "and that means."—"Dialogue" means "to say / The heart's opinion, to hear much / Of days of love / And deeds that occur." Dialogue is "to say and to hear." Yet this is only how we designate the component parts of any reciprocal discourse. The "dialogue" is distinctive by virtue of what is said and what is heard there. What is essential is what attunes the saying and heard voice. From here the manner of saying and hearing is at the same time determined.

To be said is "the heart's opinion." If we were to equate opinion with "view" here, then we would not hit upon the truth of this turn of phrase. "Saying the opinion" does not here mean expressing one's own view about something. A connection has been made, presumably correctly, between the word *Meinung* and *Minne* [courtly love]. What is opined is here that toward which our intent is directed. Whence "the heart's opinion"—that which the heart, namely, the "holy mourning" one, "wants." Such is that to which the heart is resolved in its very ground, that without which it is not, and cannot be, what it is. What is here opined in the heart is the holy, which itself only ever is historically in the encountering of humans and gods. What is thus opined is that toward which the heart thinks in advance and steadfastly. What is thus thought is that wherein the heart clings and which it "wants" from its very ground.

What is thought, opined, and "wanted" in this sense is then that wherein all wishing gathers itself. "Wishing" in this essential sense is different from mere desiring, which in each case wants what it desires only for itself, and in so doing wants only itself: the unleashed vanity of one's own "ego" that avoids all that is fitting. Such wishing, admittedly, is itself vain and empty, without correct thinking and therefore without understanding. Concerning this "wishing," Hölderlin says in the third strophe of the hymn "The Rhine" (IV, 173):

> Doch unverständig ist
> Das Wünschen vor dem Schiksaal.

> Yet uncomprehending is
> Wishing in the face of destiny.

By contrast, wishing in the sense of the "willing" that wants what the heart opines, and as the heart opines it, is comprehending, and is the manner of correctly understanding, and that means, of thinking, what mortals think when they think essentially in the direction of their essence. What the heart's opinion wants, concerns destiny and the festival. Hölderlin tells of this essential "wishing" in the fragmentary and most mysterious elegy already mentioned, "The Passage to Land" (IV, 112ff.). The second strophe begins:

> Denn nicht Mächtiges ists, zum Leben aber gehört es,
> Was wir wollen, und scheint schiklich und freudig zugleich.

> For it is not something mighty, yet to life it belongs,
> What we want, and appears fitting and joyous at once.

"Not something mighty"—that is, not something magnificent or effective in making an impression, or something that exercises dominion and thereby first secures a validity for itself. Yet the not mighty is indeed by no means something paltry and inessential, but that which belongs to "life" and makes life, life. That which is wanted and opined is that which is fitting and related to destiny. This is why it also stands in the radiance of the joyous, even if the latter must from time to time be said "in mourning."

In the dialogue there is said what inceptually and pervasively attunes the heart, that into which it has fittingly destined itself. Through what is thus spoken, the dialogue itself first becomes fitting and, that is, good. What is spoken in the dialogue is, however, not exhausted in what is said. What is spoken in the dialogue is at the same time that which is heard. That which is said and that which is heard are the Same, which is why genuine hearing is indeed also an originary resaying, and not a mere repeating. Likewise, genuine saying and being able to say is in itself already a hearing. It is only because we assign saying and hearing to the mouth and ear, and because these instruments are different in appearance, that we seldom recognize that saying and hearing not only belong together but are in an essential sense the Same. Because they are such, that which is said and that which is heard must also be the Same. From this there arises the rare miracle that those who *are* in the dialogue have, again and again, everything to say to one another, and at the same time always nothing.

§54. Listening in the dialogue to love and deed, which, as celebration, ground the festival in advance

What is to be "said" in the dialogue is "the heart's opinion." What is to be "heard" in the dialogue is "much / Of days of love, / And deeds that occur." What is heard is the days of love that once were and deeds that have occurred. The hearing hears "much." The "much" in no way signifies the mere quantity of diverse things but the fullness of One. The hearing apprehends something that once was, something that occurred. What is heard, however, is not a proclamation about something past; rather, hearing hears that which once was as that which once was. Hearing becomes initiated into what once was and intimately familiar with its essence. Hearing is a being reminded of the magnanimity [*Großmut*] and gentleness [*Sanftmut*] and forbearance [*Langmut*] of the love that *has* found its way into its essence and that first prevails in its essence as something that once has been in such a manner. Hearing in the dialogue is a being reminded of the frankness [*Freimut*] and self-sacrifice [*Opfermut*] of the deed, which as something that occurred is always a consummation, and as such grounds something essential.

Love and deed fulfill the cheerfulness [*Hochgemut*] of that cheer [*Mut*] from which alone the *Gemüt* of mortals may summon from itself [*sich zumuten*] the readiness for what is its own. From the right to such summoning, freedom receives its measure, in which human beings can on each occasion historically be themselves. For only out of the freedom for what is their own and within their own can they come to be at home on the soil that is to bear their history and be the locale for their festival.

Love attunes our cheer for the festival, which is the "bridal festival." The deeds, however, are not exhausted and do not in the first instance exhaust themselves, in success or in what is effected, for they are in themselves the freeing of cheer to inhabit destiny. Love and deed in the realm of mortals are the celebration through which the festival is grounded in advance and in a certain way is poetized. Love and deeds are the poetic of the time-space in which mortals are authentically "there." This is why the poets liked to hear of love and deeds. This is why the poets themselves must also be named together with love and deeds. Hölderlin therefore speaks on occasion of "generals in times of old" and "beautiful women" and "poets" and "many men." To be reminded of such is hearing in the dialogue. And saying in the dialogue is a reminding of the Same.

For "the heart's opinion," too, is in each case the opining of what is fitting, and is reminding, is the saying of that which already prevailed in essence. As the reciprocal relation of saying and hearing, the dialogue is the reciprocal play of recalling and being reminded. The dialogue is recollection. Its play is never frivolously playful, because this play lets resonate the unity of that accord in whose realm those saying and those hearing encounter one another.

Recollection, correctly understood, is here a becoming intimately entrusted with the essential, as that which always once already prevailed in essence. That which thus prevails in essence must entrust itself to mortals of its own accord. That is its way of becoming manifest. Yet because that which entrusts itself already prevailed and prevails in essence, it always shelters within it something earlier to which it points back, yet without letting it appear. What is recollected is filled with something that at the same time withdraws and anchors recollection in that which is concealed. Becoming manifest in self-withdrawal, however, is the way in which the destiny that is historically in the festival prevails in essence, the festival whose celebration is entrusted to mortals in the form of love and deed.

We can therefore say: the dialogue that says the heart's opinion and hears of love and deeds is the preparation granted to mortals for the heavenly dialogue into which mortals must already be drawn. Only from out of this recollective being entrusted with that which has been entrusted to them can those who say and hear in the dialogue trust one another and, as trusting, be those entrusted, be friends. Entrustedness in what has thus been entrusted is, however, the sole measure of the intimate trust of the dialogue of friends. Nevertheless, the friends do not first "make" their dialogue; for what is spoken in such dialogue is what it is, that which is recollected, only if those speaking—that is, saying and hearing—are themselves already spoken to by that which, in the dialogue, is being spoken and yet never spoken out. The dialogue first "makes" the friends, brings them into their authentic essence, which they do not satisfy by themselves, and never directly. Those who speak in saying and hearing are therefore not always purely spoken to by that which, in and for recollection, has entrusted itself to them.

§55. The endangering of the poetic dialogue of love and deeds by chatter

Good, indeed, that is, fitting, is a dialogue of the kind of saying and hearing outlined. Yet such dialogue cannot always succeed. For what accomplishes itself in it in each case is the thinking of those "thoughts" of mortals through which their cheer is a cheerful one and thus suited to fulfilling, through such thinking, the peace of that gathering with which learning the free use of one's own is to begin. This, however, is after all what is most difficult. Yet if what is most difficult is that which is least secure from any attack, then the dialogue, which is recollection of the poetic as love and deeds, must be threatened by the corruption of its essence. The constant endangering of the dialogue is chatter, which always chatters in an indiscrimate manner about everything, the high and the low, and thereby would like to seize the highest and the heavens for itself, thus everywhere missing the poetic.

Let us not forget here that Hölderlin truly knows the dialogue and its re-collective poetic essence, because he knows at the same time the corrupted essence of the dialogue, and thus the constantly threatened rareness and difficulty of the essential dialogue. Among the fragments of his hymnal poetizing, we find a word that attests for us Hölderlin's knowing of the corrupted essence of the dialogue (IV, 257):

offen die Fenster des Himmels
Und freigelassen der Nachtgeist
Der himmelstürmende, der hat unser Land
Beschwäzet, mit Sprachen viel, undichtrischen, und

Den Schutt gewälzet
Bis diese Stunde.
Doch kommt das, was ich will.

                 opened the windows of the heavens
And the spirit of night set free
Storming the heavens, he reduced our land
To chatter, with many tongues, unpoetic, and
Tossed the rubble
To this very hour.
Yet there comes what I want.

What the poet wants is the fitting. This comes. Yet its coming must find an appropriate arrival. For this, according to the word of the elegy "The Walk in the Country," "the soil must be consecrated with good talk." The "many" tongues of chatter, however, toss the rubble, and instead of consecrating the soil, they lay waste to the land.

The chatter is "unpoetic." In the draft of the fragment that has been preserved, the poet attempted to clarify this word. Von Hellingrath notes the following in this regard (IV, 392, top): "over 'unpoetic' are stacked, like a tower, the variants: 'unending,' 'unpeaceful,' 'unbounded,' 'unbridled.'"

From this remark of von Hellingrath's we may surmise: the poetic is not something endless and without banks, but rather that which fits itself into what is fitting; the poetic is the peacefulness of lucid peace. The poetic is the bounded, that which binds itself and, as bound, is binding. The poetic is the measureful that remains under bridle and measure. All this, however, said of language, insofar as it is not chatter but dialogue.

As opposed to the unpoetic language of chatter, the dialogue is poetic. This essence of the dialogue alone also corresponds to the inner coherence of the third strophe, which deals with the necessity of the dialogue for the poet who gathers himself for learning the free use of one's own.

Only now has it become clear that we are not here dealing with "dialogue" in some general manner. Yet it is also superfluous to demonstrate at length that, because poetizing is not some esoteric business but the founding of what remains, this essence of the dialogue also determines in advance every genuine dialogue in its own way. The dialogue is poetic.

§56. The poetic dialogue as "remembrance"

We say the Same while specifying: the dialogue is remembrance. It places us into an entrustedness with that which already prevails in essence and, through its saying of love and hearing of deeds, makes manifest the intimacy of destiny.

The dialogue is, as this entrustedness, the essential middle of the friendship of friends. Those entrusting themselves to one another, however, are those entrusted only if they are addressed by the intimacy that has entrusted itself to their recollection. We find here the same relations that showed themselves to us in the essence of the greeting and of those who greet. Those who greet are able to greet only if, and insofar as, they are themselves those who are greeted.

In the dialogue, there is a finding oneself, in such a way that those who say and hear distance themselves from one another, insofar as they are in each case directed back toward their own essence in being spoken to and heard. This distancing is not separation but is rather that freeing of oneself through which a free and open realm emerges between those speaking, a leeway in whose play-space one's own is allowed to appear, and upon whose soil those speaking are alone able to be homely and are homely too, if they find their way into the truth of what is fitting. The form of this truth is friendship. In its essence it prevails more primordially than the friends, just as the dialogue is more primordial than those speaking. It awaits the latter, who in each case only ever let themselves enter the dialogue. The dialogue, therefore, does not only speak out the soulful thoughts, as though it were merely the belated making known of what is thought. Rather, what is thought is first thought in the dialogue. The dialogue is itself the thinking of what is fitting. And because the dialogue is recollection, this thinking [*Denken*] is therefore a "remembrance" ["*Andenken*"]. Because this thinking thinks in the manner of remembrance and never merely represents something at hand, it must at the same time think in the direction of that which is coming; it can, and on occasion even must, first prepare itself within the gathered peacefulness of those individuals who are poets and who, as poets, know of love and of deeds.

The poet awaits the coming festival, the encountering of humans and gods, an encountering in which the heavenly ones need human beings. This is why there must be those who help the heavenly ones. Only the poet, who knows what is fitting, is capable of recognizing those who are suited to be of help to the heavenly ones. This is why Hölderlin, in the hymn "The Titans," says (IV, 208ff., lines 43ff.):

> Manche helfen
> Dem Himmel. Diese siehet
> Der Dichter. Gut ist es, an andern sich
> Zu halten. Denn keiner trägt das Leben allein.

> Some help
> The heavens. These the poet
> Sees. It is good to keep
> To others. For no one bears life alone.

"It is good to keep / To others." We may now think this word more clearly if we hear the other word: "Yet good / Is a dialogue . . ."

§57. The question of where the friends are, and the essence of future friendship

Presumably a dialogue is *good*. Yet *is* it also always? Can it ever be brought about forcibly and instituted? No. It must be given. Even the individual's, and especially the poet's preparation for the dialogue, commemorative thinking, is always a bestowal, something the poet can only request. This "requesting" does not beg for a donation that replaces the festival and relieves one of preparing for it. This requesting is for the excessive demand of that which is fitting, for the hours of celebration, for the times that first precede the festival. The beginning of the hymn "The Titans" includes a sequence of lines that corresponds to the third strophe of "Remembrance," and that means at the same time, to the transition from the third to the fourth strophe:

> Indessen, gieb in Feierstunden
> Und dass ich ruhen möge, der Todten
> Zu denken. Viele sind gestorben
> Feldherrn in alter Zeit
> Und schöne Frauen und Dichter
> Und in neuer
> Der Männer viel.
> Ich aber bin allein.

> Still, in hours of celebration
> And that I might rest, give thought
> To the dead. Many have died
> Generals in ancient times
> And beautiful women and poets
> And in recent times
> Many men.
> But I am alone.

This last line "But I am alone" names the ground for the question with which the fourth strophe of "Remembrance" begins. Because the poet is alone, he asks:

> Wo aber sind die Freunde? Bellarmin
> Mit dem Gefährten? . . .
> . . . . . .

> Yet where are the friends? Bellarmine
> And companion? . . .
>
> . . . . . .

This question is the sole question in the poem, and is perhaps even *the* question of the poem. The question concerning the friends is asked directly in this way, as though the friends had hitherto always been thought of already. Indeed they have been thought of, too, even though nothing has been said explicitly of them. For what is thought of in the naming of the dialogue and naming of the fact that it is good, is the friendship of friends. The friends are thought of already in greeting the land of Greece. The friendship already exists, but it remains to be asked where the friends are.

However, the same strophe surely makes known at the same time where they are, in saying who they are, what they do, and how they comport themselves. Then the question "Yet where are the friends?" would not, therefore, be a serious question at all, but more just the linguistic form of ascertaining that the friends are not there, which indeed is why the poet is "alone."

Yet is the poet alone only because the friends are not there, or are the friends not yet "there" because the poet is alone? The latter hits upon the essential. The poet is the only one who has already come home into his own, in such a way that, in greeting, he thinks of that which once was. With this "remembrance," however, the dialogue has in essence already begun. The friends are not "there," that is to say, they are not at that place to which the poet has gone over and from which he is greeting. The friends are not in the realm of the homely and of one's own; more precisely, they are not on the path of learning, in which the free use of one's own is to be appropriated. That the friends are friends does not yet guarantee that they are able to freely use the homely and, out of original friendship, measure up to what constituted the need of their native homeland. Thus, the friends have remained behind outside of the realm of the homely, in the foreign. By his transition to the homely, the poet has left them behind in the foreign land, where he himself was previously, and where he sought what is "properly authentic" in the foreign, without giving thought to his own.

Back then he was a young Greek named Hyperion in the land of Greece. Back then there was already a dialogue in the form of letters that he wrote to his friend. Hölderlin's poetic work *Hyperion; or, The Hermit in Greece* is presented in the form of letters. The one who receives the majority of the letters is called "Bellarmine."

> Wo aber sind die Freunde? Bellarmin
> Mit dem Gefährten?
>
> Yet where are the friends? Bellarmine
> And companion?

The naming of this name points back to the poet's previous journey. At the same time, it betrays the fact that the poet surely knows where the friends are. So why, then, still raise the question of where they are? If the question "Yet where are . . ." were merely supposed to inquire into the locale where the friends reside, then the question would indeed be superfluous. The linguistic turn of phrase would merely be a sham question expressing an answer that had already been decided. The question, however, is a genuine question. How so? We merely fail to give sufficient thought to what is being asked about.

"Yet where are the friends . . . ?" The question, as a genuine one, surely presupposes that the friends are not there. Where not there? Not in the neighborhood of Hölderlin who stays at home, not in the Swabian homeland? No and yes. The question is ambiguous. Where are they not there? Not there, where now a dialogue is good, not there, where now, following the transition over the footbridge, a dialogue is necessary and possible. The dialogue in the sense named here accomplishes the beginning of the gathering of thought in the direction of learning the free use of one's own. For this, it is not enough that those who are to talk with one another are indeed present in general. They must, if this expression is allowed here, "take their post," that is, be ready for that which the locale demands of them. Ready for the locale: that is to say, open and inclined toward its essence. The essence of the present stay is not simply the homeland as a landscape present before us, but coming to be at home as the passage to one's own.

The question "Yet where are the friends?" asks whether the friends are themselves already underway on the passage to what is their own, or whether their path goes in a different direction. The interrogative "where?" is not simply asking about a geographical locale, but about the essential manner of their stay and, that is, about the way in which the friends are "there." Insofar as the poet must still ask this, however, this tells us that the friends have not yet attained the essential manner in which a peaceful dialogue is to be accomplished. More than that, the essence of the stay required for the dialogue, and thereby the essence of the dialogue, remains worthy of questioning.

The question "Yet where are the friends?" is accordingly meant to assist in determining more originarily what the essence of this dialogue of the friends is that is supposed to prepare a future "heavenly dialogue." This dialogue of the friends is "remembrance," but remembrance as the beginning of learning, as the passage to appropriating one's own.

The question of the friends is the question of the essence of future friendship. Within the realm of this friendship, the poet is himself also a friend. What the fourth strophe asks indeed deals with the friends, yet also surely concerns the poet, indeed him first of all. This is what we must thoughtfully heed in order not to misinterpret what ensues as something the poet is teaching us about others, from whom he could be excluded. Precisely because the question concerning the friends stands so decisively and singularly within the poem as a whole, the danger lies near that we may choose an inappropriate level for determining the different essential locales of the friends and of the poet.

§58. The friends' being shy to go to the source

The question "Yet where are the friends?" does not appear to be followed directly by an answer, but initially by an observation concerning the comportment of the friends:

> Mancher
> Trägt Scheue, an die Quelle zu gehn;

> Many a one
> Is shy of going to the source;

Is that just a word concerning the comportment of the friends? Is it not, rather, the authentic, therefore poetic, response to the question? There is a veiled bearing witness to the fact that the friends are not "there"; thus, there is unveiled what the essence of the locale is where the friends are not, yet to which the poet is underway. "Many a one / Is shy of going to the source"; this says the Same as the word from the hymn "The Titans":

> Ich aber bin allein.

> But I am alone.

Yet this does not mean: I am the only one who has comprehended the passage to the homely and the necessity of such passage. The "I" does not puff itself up here into an exception among the poets, as though to point out to those remaining the superiority of being the "only one" and at the same time to impute to the others a lack of courage [Mut] and insight. The word means nothing whatsoever of the kind. Rather, it unveils the difficulty of conceding that one stands oneself at the beginning of what is most difficult. The word is neither accusation nor disparagement. It wants neither to reproach nor to insist on one's own "poetic achievement." The word betrays nothing of the presumption of being the self-assured exception that often erupts in Nietzsche. The word attests to the awe of the first sacrificed before the sacrifice.

"Many a one / Is shy . . ." To these "many" there belongs in the first instance, and even now following his transition to the other side, the poet who says this word. It seals the friendship of the friends, who are friends to one another on the grounds of their belonging to the same vocation: to be the poets of the transition. The word that seals friendship within the domain of future poets must, as the word of a friend, be at once severe and mild:

> Mancher
> Trägt Scheue, an die Quelle zu gehn;

> Many a one
> Is shy of going to the source;

"Many a one": this does not merely mean "lots," yet nor does it mean "a few," but rather someone on occasion, and always again someone on some occasion. These "many" are "sometimes." Their "time" corresponds to the while of destiny that has been equalized. "Many a one" does not refer to a "number," but to being chosen by destiny. "Many a one"—these are the ones called upon, whose passage is sealed by awe. "Many a one," that is to say, including the one that I myself am. These, whose essence receives such a seal, carry within themselves, in the middle of their heart, the center of gravity that is shyness.

What is that—shyness? Presumably something other than timidity. The latter, in everything it encounters, only ever remains apprehensive and uncertain everywhere. Shyness, by contrast, is magnetized by the unequivocally singular thing in the face of which it is shy. Shyness is not in any way uncertain, and yet keeps to itself. Yet this keeping to itself on the part of shyness does not become entangled in worry about itself, unlike fearfulness. The keeping to itself that pertains to shyness, however, also never knows reservation. Shyness, as an originarily steadfast keeping to oneself in the face of that before which one is shy, is at the same time the most intimate inclining toward the latter. That which attunes us to shyness lets us hesitate. Yet the hesitation belonging to shyness does not know apprehensiveness or despair. The hesitation belonging to shyness is a waitful resolve to patience; hesitation is the long-since-decided, long-drawn-out courage [*lange Mut*] for what is long and slow; hesitation is forbearance [*Langmut*]. Yet shyness does not exhaust its essence in such hesitation, but is more originary than this.

For what essentially prevails in shyness before all else is an inclining toward that before which one is shy, an inclining whose intimate familiarity veils itself in remaining distant and that holds whatever is distant near to it in casting its astonishment over toward it. Shyness is a thinking that keeps to itself, fulfilling itself and inclined with forbearance in the direction of that which is near, in a nearness that is singularly taken up with keeping distant something distant in its fullness and thereby keeping it constantly ready in its springing forth. Essential shyness is the attunement of a far-seeing thinking of the origin. Shyness is the center of gravity in which the heart of those poets must repose who in this way bring the course of history belonging to a particular humankind into what is homely for it. Shyness does not inhibit, but it sets the long and slow upon its path and is thus the attunement for the footbridges. It attunes the going and directs it toward the passage into what is originary.

Shyness emerges and awakens only where something distant appears as the sole thing to which those who are distanced in an inceptual manner authentically belong. What is thus distant initially shows itself as the foreign. The foreign is strange and disconcerting. Yet shyness is not shyness in the face of that which disconcerts, but in the face of what is one's own and intimately entrusted from afar, that which begins to light up within the foreign as the foreign.

§59. "Source" and "river." The wealth of the origin

Of what are those friends shy who are marked by shyness? Of the passage to the source. Therein lies: seen in relation to the most distant thing of which it is shy, that is, in relation to what is nearest and authentic for it, shyness is shyness before *the source itself*. What does "source" mean here?

Source means many things. The poet leaves the word vague and indeterminate. So it may seem, so long as we hear only this isolated line and fail to ponder thoughtfully the whole poem in terms of the ground of that which it poetizes. What it poetizes is the one thing for which the entire hymnal poetizing seeks the word.

"Source" is the origin from which there springs the flowing and coursing waters. These waters are the rivers. Of them it is said:

> Umsonst nicht gehn
> Im Troknen die Ströme. Aber wie? Sie sollen nemlich
> Zur Sprache seyn.

> Not in vain do
> Rivers run in the dry. Yet how? Namely, they are
> To be to language.

This word concerning the rivers is found in a hymn, namely, in the hymn "The Ister" ("The Danube") (IV, 221).

A second hymn with this name has been preserved for us: "At the Source of the Danube." The two Danube hymns and the Rhine hymn bring into the word the language of the "waters of the homeland" of "Germania." More than all other rivers, the Danube is the river of the poet's homeland. (However, one scarcely needs a lengthy discussion, presumably, to fend off the misunderstanding that Hölderlin is here a "poet of the Swabian homeland." This worthy vocation has its own enjoyment and legitimacy.) The Danube hymn "At the Source of the Danube" names in its title the more local area of the Upper Swabian homeland of the poet. "At the Source of the Danube" is a naming of the river whose source is "to language" for the essential dialogue in which the event of the encountering of humans and gods will in the future be decided and come to pass:

> Mancher
> Trägt Scheue, an die Quelle zu gehn;

> Many a one
> Is shy of going to the source;

"The source"—that is the origin of the waters of the homeland, whose course speaks of the homeland as the soil that is to be consecrated for the festival. The source, however, names that which is originarily indigenous to the homeland, that which is authentically one's own. To find one's way there and to take up free residence in the free realm of the homeland is what is most difficult. "Many a one / is shy" of going to the origin. Yet what if someone were once to make this passage and henceforth dwelled in nearness to the source? Then what is most difficult would be overcome. Certainly, insofar as it refers to the difficulty of the free use of one's own. And yet, one's ownmost and the origin retain difficulty within them; only it now appears transformed, insofar as now, for one who *has* once gone to the source, it is abandoning the homely locale that is, by converse, difficult, if it does not indeed become impossible. This is why Hölderlin also says a counterword to "Many a one / Is shy to go to the source." It is found in the hymn "The Journey" and reads (IV, 167):

> Schwer verlässt
> Was nahe dem Ursprung wohnet, den Ort.

> With difficulty that
> Which dwells near the origin abandons the locale.

"At the source" means the locale in the neighborhood of the origin. To dwell here means to be a good neighbor to the ownmost of one's own. One's own-most is never a possession—it is one's ownmost only as sought in a seeking. Seeking is now more precisely: the passage to the source. It is because many a one is shy of this that the friends are not there, not homely in the home-land. On account of this shyness, however, the poet too is himself not yet homely, even though he has gone over the footbridge.

With the return home, authentic becoming homely first begins, for one's ownmost is the origin, and the origin is the inexhaustible. From the source there indeed flows the pure fullness of one's ownmost. Yet is this fullness therefore also already found directly "at the source"? Can someone in general ever directly be "at" the source? What if the source initially were to point precisely away from itself, in the direction of the river flowing from it? Then going to the source would be almost counter to its sense. This is why it is also the most difficult thing to approach the source in accordance with its realm.

The source closes off one's own. Everything genuinely owned, how-ever, that is, that for whose "possession" we are properly suited, is in itself wealth. Why is the finding and appropriating of this wealth what is most difficult? Surely we already possess what is our own. It is, after all, our authentic and singular wealth. Certainly—but it is difficult, and the most difficult thing, to be wealthy in this wealth. For only one who has first become poor, in the sense of a poverty that is not deprivation, can be wealthy and use such wealth. Deprivation always remains a not-having that would like to "have" everything directly, just as directly as it does not have, yet without being properly suited for it. Such deprivation does not arise from the courage [Mut] of poverty [Armut]. The deprivation that wants to have is a wretchedness that is unceasingly fixated on wealth, without being able to know or wanting to take on its genuine essence and the conditions for appropriating it. Essential, originary poverty is the courage for the simple and originary that does not need to be fixated on something. This poverty catches sight of the essence of wealth and therefore knows its law and the manner in which it offers itself. In this, the essence of wealth conceals itself. Such wealth does not, therefore, let itself be appropriated directly.

Being wealthy must be learned. Only the essential poverty knows that genuine wealth wants to be learned. The learning must begin where the wealth shows itself most readily. Initially, however, the wealth shows itself where it is spread out. For in being spread out it initially offers itself, because this offering demands only a mere accepting and drawing from it, at first relieving us of all appropriating or even seeking. The wealth of the source is spread out where the river itself that has sprung from it has spread itself out, and where, as river, it "spreads" "into the ocean." Here the wealth begins:

> Es beginnet nemlich der Reichtum
> Im Meere.

> For wealth indeed begins
> In the ocean.

The river has gone out into the ocean. The river itself "is" the source in such a manner, namely, the water that is "propelled from its very origin" (V, 273). In the ocean, into which the river has flowed and spread out, the source conceals itself and yet spreads itself out in it and extends itself. The sea is therefore of a peculiar ambiguity for the commemorative passage to one's own. The ocean is the beginning of the offering of wealth. This beginning, however, is not the commencement. To commence from the commencement, that is, the origin, is what comes last. Only in what comes last in this way does that which is first and singular authentically prevail.

The initial task, therefore, is to go away from the source, downstream, in the direction of the river's flowing out, to set out upon the ocean. Away from the source, that is, away from the homeland into the foreign.

§60. The initial appropriation of "wealth" on the poets' voyage across the ocean into the foreign

The stay in the foreign and alienation in the foreign must be, in order for one's own to begin to light up in relation to the foreign. This distant lighting up awakens a remote inclining toward one's own. Hesitation begins. Forbearance becomes strong. Shyness attunes and permeates all comportment. The seeking of one's own has found its essential ground. It is not some self-centered, unfettered groping around. Through shyness, the seeking of one's own is in advance delivered over to the remoteness of one's own. The voyage across the ocean thus stands under the concealed law of the return home to one's own.

Who are these mariners who initially appropriate the wealth of the originary for themselves on their voyage across the ocean? Who are the companions from the poetic period when *Hyperion* is poetized?

> Sie,
> Wie Maler, bringen zusammen
> Das Schöne der Erd' . . .

They,
Like painters, bring together
The beautiful of the Earth . . .

The ocean voyagers are of the nature of painters; they "bring together," in Greek: συνάγειν; in Latin: *componere*. They do not simply copy what is beautiful on Earth. The beautiful never lets itself be copied at all; it must be "composed." The ocean voyagers are *like* painters in their bringing together. They are not themselves painters, for those who are being referred to are the companions of the *poet*, therefore themselves poets. What is the beautiful that these poets "bring together" and, that is, gather back to the unity of the One?

The beautiful is here not some pleasing or charming thing that is collected. "The beautiful of the Earth" is the Earth in its beauty; it refers to beauty itself. For Hölderlin, during the period when *Hyperion* is poetized, this is the name for "beyng." In place of many pieces of evidence, we cite one excerpt from a draft, first discovered in 1920, of a preface to *Hyperion* (II, 546):

> To end that eternal conflict between our self and the world, to restore the peace of all peace, which is higher than all reason, to unite ourselves with nature, into One infinite whole: that is the goal of all our striving, whether we agree about it or not.
>
> Yet neither our knowledge nor our action at any period of existence attains that point where all conflict ceases, where All is One; a determinate line can be united with an indeterminate one only in infinite approximation.
>
> We would also have no intimation of that infinite peace, of that beyng, in the singular sense of the word, we would not strive at all to unite nature with ourselves, we would not think and would not act, there would be nothing at all, (for us) we ourselves would think nothing, (for us) unless through that infinite unification, that beyng, in the singular sense of the word, were present for us. It is present—as beauty; to speak with Hyperion, a new kingdom awaits us, where beauty will be queen.—
>
> I believe in the end we shall all say: holy Plato, forgive! one has [originally: "we have"] sinned against you mightily.
>
> The Editor.

Beauty, as beyng, can be brought into view only by συναγωγή—by bringing together into One, not by a random copying of facts. Bringing together does not first bring about the One, but rather already has this One in view as that which unifies and brings it to appear in its unifying. The One is that which rests in itself, that which is regal in "queen" "beauty." The analogy with the painters is meant to indicate that in this bringing together, the projection of the One and what underlies it, ὑπόθεσις, remains what is essential. The poets, as it is put in the same preface, are not "reporters," those who run after the mere alternation of ever new "facts."

The analogy between the poets and painters by no means wants to speak in favor of "descriptive poesy." That Hölderlin clearly rejects the latter is shown by a distich that was composed immediately after *Hyperion*, and that still points back to this period (III, 6):

> Wisst! Apoll ist der Gott der Zeitungsschreiber geworden,
> Und sein Mann ist wer ihm treulich das Faktum erzählt.

> Know this! Apollo has become the god of journalists,
> And his man is whoever faithfully narrates him the facts.

The poets do not report, they project the image, and in it bring into view the visage that constitutes the outward look, the ἰδέα of beings. They must, however, experience this on their voyage, out of the manifold of appearances on Earth. They must ascend from the totality of beings toward being.

(That the poets are here thought "like painters" contains the concealed truth about the essence of the poetic vocation of the poets who have not yet transitioned over to the other side. They are poets within the essential realm of "metaphysics.")

For this, it is necessary that they experience much, and in coming to know the foreign, withstand its perils and through confrontation with it test their own ability:

>   und verschmähn
> Den geflügelten Krieg nicht,

>   and do not spurn
> The winged war,

Their war is called winged after "the ship's wings," the word that Hölderlin uses in the elegy "The Archipelago" to name the sails (IV, 91, line 81). The "winged war" is the struggle with the adversity of the winds and unfavorable weather. Such struggle discloses for the first time the wealth that begins in the ocean. During this struggle the poets do not dwell near to the origin but rather are resolved:

> Zu wohnen einsam, jahrlang, unter
> Dem entlaubten Mast . . .

> To dwell in solitude, year long, beneath
> The defoliate mast . . .

§61. The "year long" learning of the foreign on the ocean voyage of a long time without festival

They are to learn to use the foreign, but they are not permitted to become homely in it. Neither in the foreign nor in what is their own are they at home. The ocean voyage and their stay in the foreign do not pass quickly by, as though all this were merely an episode that could be taken lightly: the beginning of learning the foreign, a learning that must first precede the authentic learning of one's own, lasts "year long." Here, nothing can be rushed, and nothing can be forcibly brought about at the unpropitious time.

The time of the voyage beneath the mast is like a long winter, in which the trees are left without foliage and the forces and juices of growth hold back. The mast, with its woodwork and rigging, sways in the storm like a tree without its leaves in winter. The poet knows that preparing for the passage to the source and for the appropriation of one's own origin is a time of far-reaching decisions. The transition and the footbridges are slow; the time is a time of night. The night is the time before the day, which as holiday yet itself remains the day before the festival. During this time that far precedes the festival, the companions voyage:

> wo nicht die Nacht durchglänzen
> Die Feiertage der Stadt,
> Und Saitenspiel und eingeborener Tanz nicht.

> where there gleam not through the night
> The holidays of the town,
> Nor the music of strings nor native dance.

(cf. p. 60 above)

Yet must not the voyage in such nighttime be an errant one, after all? What possibilities still remain here, other than sheer adventure? The adventurer has placed "his stake on nothing," which here means, on his sole pleasure. To him, the foreign is the alien, the exotic, which in his desire for intoxication he samples fleetingly, so as to perhaps thereby experience the shock of the surprising and unusual, which he then equates with the wonderful. Yet the ocean voyage of the companions of the poet, who has made the transition to the other side, is of a different gravity than the adventure: it is noble and sober. The sea voyage of the companions knows the foreign not as the excitement of the exotic, but as the first glimmer of one's own. The night is a "holy night" because it already requires staying awake in awaiting the holy.

The figure of the adventurer is possible only within the historical space of the humankind of modernity and its "subjectivity." Odysseus was not yet an adventurer. The seafarers referred to, that is, poetized by Hölderlin are no longer adventurers. The "adventurous heart"[4] belongs in the realm of the metaphysics of the will to power. Not so the heart of Hölderlin's companions. Their heart bears shyness. This ocean voyage is the clear crossing of a long time without festival. The length of time contains the guarantee that the true comes to pass. This long time is the time-space of a concealed history. No modern thinking, indeed no metaphysics in general, suffices to experience, let alone to know this history. Because, however, our own thought and action is everywhere metaphysical, we cannot yet find our way into the historical space of this history. We ourselves must first learn something *still more* provisional, waiting for the favor of being able to await authentically the long time. Such waiting, certainly, does not consist in the empty waiting for some stroke of fortune that will supposedly throw salvation our way, toward those of us who are entirely unprepared. Waiting for the favor of being able to await the long time is reflection. Reflection is readiness for knowing.

Only *one* path leads to Hölderlin's knowing of the historicality of history; that is the path whose signpost Hölderlin himself placed in his poetizing at distant intervals. The unfinished hymn "Mnemosyne" contains the word (IV, 225):

> Lang ist
> Die Zeit, es ereignet sich aber
> Das Wahre.

> Long is
> The time, yet what is true
> Comes to pass.

The mariners must wait through this "long time," in which for an extended time and ever again anew it "is *not* yet time," and must practice forbearance. (Forbearance [*Langmut*] is not empty and impassive waiting, but the courage for what is long [*der Mut zum Langen*], for that which reaches over into the coming festival.) Even the poet, who has returned home from the voyage, cannot cast off forbearance. He remains a companion to his companions and waits for the dialogue and for the ability to say, even when and precisely when, from time to time, he is cheered by musical strings from his homeland that "play something loving." Indeed, for him forbearance first becomes manifest in its essence as that which lets the long time of waiting and the retaining of what once was truly endure and prevail in

---

4 Ernst Jünger, *Das abenteuerliche Herz. Aufzeichnungen bei Tag und Nacht* (Berlin, 1929); second version, *Das abenteuerliche Herz. Figuren und Capriccios* (1938). Translated by Thomas Friese as *The Adventurous Heart: Figures and Capriccios* (Candor, NY: Telos Press, 2012).

their essence. This steadfast insistence within the originary historical time of essential history is care.

(The adventurous human being can comprehend care only as weakness and worry, since he thinks only subjectively, that is, metaphysically, and supposedly loves severity. If the latter fails, he takes refuge in some kind of intoxication, if only that of frenzy.)

To be "there" in the essential ground of care is the concealed calling of the few—or at first only that of a single human being.

The elegy "Homecoming" closes thus (IV, 107ff.):

> Schweigen müssen wir oft; es fehlen heilige Nahmen,
> Herzen schlagen und doch bleibet die Rede zurük?
> Aber ein Saitenspiel leiht jeder Stunde die Töne,
> Und erfreuet vieleicht Himmlische, welche sich nahn.
> Das bereitet und so ist auch beinahe die Sorge
> Schon befriediget, die unter das Freudige kam.
> Sorgen, wie diese, muss, gern oder nicht, in der Seele
> Tragen ein Sänger und oft, aber die anderen nicht.

> We must often be silent; holy names are lacking,
> Hearts beat, yet still our talk holds back?
> But a playing of musical strings lends each hour its tones,
> And perhaps cheers heavenly ones, who draw near.
> That prepares and thus is care also almost
> Already put at ease, as it came under the cheerful.
> Cares such as these, willingly or not, a singer must bear
> In his soul and often, but others not.

Long is the time in which what is fitting must be sought. What is fitting is one's own, to which a humankind that belongs historically to destiny must be delivered over.

(Long and varied for individuals is the voyage. Time and again, however, the knowledge is needed of where those seeking are in their voyage, of what the essence of the locale is, to which they have gone; for each time the passage to one's own is a coming from the remoteness of the foreign, and even in the homeland itself the homely remains difficult to find after the foreign has been learned and withstood in its essence. Always, and here too, there remains a shyness to go to the source and to freely appropriate that free comportment that is appropriate to the source.)

What is their own for the Germans is the clarity of presentation. What is meant is poetizing. Yet "clarity of presentation" is not equivalent to the superficially considered feature of the understandability of what a statement is communicating. "Clarity of presentation" is the luminous and light, and that means, the open, in which the poetizing word attains and sets up that which is to be said.

§62. The singular remembrance of the locale of the friends and of the fitting that is to be poetized

"Clarity of presentation" here signifies the essence of the truth of the poetic. The poetic, however, is the essential ground for the way in which the human being dwells upon this Earth, in order that he may be at home in what is his own. "Free use" therefore also refers to something other than merely the unconstrained employment of a tool. "Free use" means to stand openly in the open realm of the essence of poetizing and its truth, and thereby to know what it is that is to be poetized.

Learning to freely use one's own is in the first instance the task given to the poets. They must find that which is fitting in their saying and be resolute in the essence of this saying. What, therefore, is the fundamental trait of presenting as setting forth, and from where is its clarity determined?

The poets who are still on their ocean voyage and on foreign coasts bring together the beautiful (beyng) like painters. Manifestly, however, the poets who have come home, who are to sing the holy of the fatherland, can no longer poetize in such a way. Yet nor can they arbitrarily invent the way that is proper to the homely; the presentation must be appropriate to that which is to be presented. One's own must be found and "experienced" as measure. The passage to the source must begin with the voyage across the ocean. Those who have come home, therefore, cannot simply put their previous voyage behind them. The voyage must carry to full term its own essence, so that it returns *as* a voyage to the foreign, returning to the source and to arrival in the homeland, and to becoming homely in this homeland.

This is why the question "Yet where are the friends?" must always also be asked as the question "Where am I myself as their friend?" This one, unified question is now more unequivocally the question of the passage to the source, and that means at the same time the question of where the friends and the questioning poet himself are underway to, and where they have gone, where they are headed on their passage.

Thinking of the friends, where they have gone to, and thinking of what is first to be attained in all this, thinking of one's own, thus coalesce in the thinking of a singular "remembrance." This "remembrance" is at once a thinking back and a thinking ahead, and always a thinking on the passage to one's own and its free use:

> Nun aber sind zu Indiern
> Die Männer gegangen,

Dort an der luftigen Spiz'
An Traubenbergen, wo herab
Die Dordogne kommt
Und zusammen mit der prächt'gen
Garonne meerbreit
Ausgehet der Strom . . .

But now to Indians
The men have gone,
There on the breezy headland
On vineyard slopes, where down
Comes the Dordogne
And together with the magnificent
Garonne the river
Spreads into the ocean . . .

The land that was greeted in the first and second strophes appears once more. "The beautiful Garonne" is again named. This southern land and its fire stands for the land of Greece.

Is that not an arbitrary interpretation? To ward off this suspicion, we must repeatedly recall the letter to Böhlendorff of December 2, 1802. Yet also the letter of December 4, 1801, prior to the journey to southern France, speaks of the land of Greece as the "Apollonian kingdom." That is the kingdom of the heavenly fire, for which Homer had to appropriate sobriety for himself as something foreign to the Greeks. After his return from France, Hölderlin speaks of the "powerful element," of the "fire from the heavens," and of his being "struck by Apollo" there.

In the poem "Remembrance," southern France stands poetically for the land of Greece. Yet in the meantime, the poet himself has gone from there to the source. Yet where have the friends gone?

Nun aber sind zu Indiern
Die Männer gegangen,

But now to Indians
The men have gone,

To "Indians"? To the Indus? Thus still further away from what, for the poet, is the land of his home. Still further away, if we measure the remoteness numerically in terms of distance. Nonetheless nearer, if we ponder the essential, the passage to the source, the arrival in Germania. It is already enigmatic enough that in *Hyperion*, the young Greek of this name is suddenly abandoned by his older male friend Adamas, after the latter has "initiated" the younger one "now . . . into Plutarch's world of heroes, now into the magic land of the Greek gods" (II, 98). Hyperion writes to his friend Bellarmine about it (II, 102):

> It looks as though I was angry with my Adamas for abandoning me, but I am not angry with him. Oh, he indeed wanted to come again! In the depths of Asia there is supposedly hidden a people of rare excellence; to them his hope drove him onward.

To the Indians by the Indus? As if the distant provenance of Germania were at the Indus and the parents of our native homeland had come from there. In the fragment of a hymn that von Hellingrath has given the title "The Eagle" we read (IV, 223):

> Anfänglich aber sind
> Aus Wäldern des Indus
> Starkduftenden
> Die Eltern gekommen.

> Yet in the beginning
> From forests of the Indus
> Strongly fragrant ones
> Our parents have come.

"Indus," in the realm of the hymnal poetry, is the poetic name for the primordial homeland, which, however, nonetheless remains remote. It is only for those who are homely and for those who seek what is their own, in such a way that they have gone there, yet at the same time returned from the Indus. Those who have returned home are who they are as those arrived from afar. However, just as the voyage of departure away from the source into the foreign and remote requires the river that spreads out into the ocean, so, too, the river, in which the source streams inexhaustibly and conceals itself, must be the sign and the path for the return.

This can be only the properly homely river of this poet: the Danube, the Ister. This is why we read in the first strophe of the hymn "The Ister" (IV, 220):

> Wir singen aber vom Indus her
> Fernangekommen . . .

> We, however, sing from the Indus
> Arrived from afar . . .

*§63. The word regarding the river that goes backwards: the shy
intimation of the essence of commencement and history*

The arrival of those who have arrived from afar, from the most distant yet
authentic remoteness of the distant origin, must follow that river which has
its source in the native homeland. If those arriving from afar who are going
to the source thus follow the river, then the river will carry them back to
the source. The river itself goes backwards, as it were. The third strophe
of the same hymn that speaks of the Indus, "The Ister," says the following
regarding the water of the homeland, the river called the Danube:

> Der scheinet aber fast
> Rükwärts zu gehen und
> Ich mein, er müsse kommen
> Von Osten.

> He appears, however, almost
> To go backwards and
> I presume he must come
> From the East.

In this mysterious word concerning the backwards flowing river of the
homeland there lies concealed everything that the poet knows and thinks
regarding the grounding and appropriation of one's own. Only the most
distant remoteness corresponds to the nearness to one's ownmost. The
source streams and *is* the source as the river that spreads out into the ocean
and thus *is* the ocean. The ocean itself *is* the source in its most distant
removal. The river is the source and is the ocean.

The word regarding the river's going backwards is not a mere illusion
or an image. The river in truth goes backwards—but this truth is the
truth of the essential, which runs contrary to everything merely correct
and ascertainable, just like the river, which, considered correctly, surely
only flows away from the source, after all. The word regarding the
backwards flowing river is the shy intimation of the concealed essence
of the commencement and of history. The latter has its essence in destiny,
which, equalized in the festival, tarries a while. Destiny presents itself only
in that which is fitting; the latter must be sought. This seeking must wait
it out in the time that is long, and must take the course of the mysterious
course of the river that is the river of the homeland:

> Wir singen aber vom Indus her
> Fernangekommen und

Vom Alpheus, lange haben
Das Schikliche wir gesucht,

We, however, sing from the Indus
Arrived from afar and
From Alpheus, long have
We sought what is fitting,

Because this seeking and taking the course of the backwards flowing river
is the secret of history, the wealth of this mystery cannot be comprehended
in a single thought or a single word in the manner of some clever artifice
and enunciated like the solution to a puzzle. This is why Hölderlin adds to
that word concerning the "river" the equally mysterious word that recurs in
different variations during the "hymnal period," and that here reads:

Vieles wäre
Zu sagen davon.

There would be
Much to tell of this.

In the Donau hymn "The Ister," the lines connected to this that tell of the
river going backwards read:

Der scheinet aber fast
Rükwärts zu gehen und
Ich mein, er müsse kommen
Von Osten.
Vieles wäre
Zu sagen davon.

He appears, however, almost
To go backwards and
I presume he must come
From the East.
There would be
Much to tell of this.

When Hölderlin in the concluding strophe of "Remembrance" thinks of
the men who have gone to the Indians, then this remembrance is a thinking
of that which is "inceptual," from which, arriving from there and solely in
the manner of arrival, those seeking can ask concerning what is homely in

their homeland and find it in its essence. That, for the Germans, is what is fitting in their destiny. The same concluding strophe of the poem "Remembrance," the strophe that at its beginning thinks still further over beyond the southern land to the supreme remoteness of the Indus, therefore tells in its last lines of one's own and of the sole way in which it may be found and preserved:

> Es nehmet aber
> Und giebt Gedächtniss die See,
> Und die Lieb' auch heftet fleissig die Augen.
> Was bleibet aber, stiften die Dichter.

> Yet what takes
> And gives memory is the sea,
> And love too fixes with intensity our eyes.
> Yet what remains, the poets found.

Even if, following all of this, we are capable of thoughtfully reflecting on Hölderlin's knowledge of the essence of history only in its vague outlines, we must meanwhile intimate in the essence of historicality caught sight of by Hölderlin a fundamental trait whose mystery gives us to think anew everything noted thus far.

History essentially prevails in destiny. Destiny tarries a while, equalized in the festival. This is prepared in the holidays. In the form that they take, the homely flourishes. The festival is the bridal festival in the manner of the encountering of humans and gods (cf. Review, p. 68). The attuning fundamental attunement of the festive is love. Yet it is not the only one.

For the most part, however, destiny remains unequalized. Gods and humans are not homely within what is homely for them, and because they are not homely [unheimisch], they are therefore also uncanny [unheimlich]. To those who are unhomely, it remains undecided what is foreign and what is one's own. Neither the one nor the other has been found. For not just one's own, but the foreign too must be learnt. If the free use of one's own is indeed what is most difficult, then this entails that withstanding the test of the foreign also remains difficult and has its own exigency. This is why Hölderlin says in his letter to Böhlendorff (December 4, 1801): "Yet one's own must be learned just as well as the foreign" (V, 320). To finding one's own there belongs the sea voyage. The attuning fundamental attunement for the festival is just as much the voyage and the deed, only in another manner than love.

§64. The passage to the foreign, "bold forgetting" of one's own, and the return home

That destiny is for the most part unequalized entails the essential need to prepare the equalization. To this there belongs the care for the mediate, within which alone the immediate appears, which is given immediately neither to gods nor to humans. The unequalized, unhomely, is not a defective state, but rather belongs to the essential state of gods and humans. This entails that human beings are historically precisely not at home at the commencement, but that their thinking and reflecting, because it seeks the homely, is before that directed precisely toward the foreign.

"Spirit loves colony." With this relation we touch upon the mystery of history and of the commencement. The commencement does not commence with the commencement. The human being too is historically not immediately in the center of his being.

The human being "traverses" an "excentric orbit." The first version of *Hyperion* already begins with this thought (II, 53). In the first draft of the Preface to the final version, we read: "We all traverse an excentric orbit, and there is no other way possible from childhood to consummation" (II, 545). This thought of the excentricity of the human essence is admittedly not the same as the more originary thinking through of the essence of history that gives the hymnal poetizing its substratum.

The knowledge among poets and thinkers concerning this mystery, like all knowledge of what is supremely concealed, is spoken only seldom, and when it is, then for the most part only in passing, in an interim remark, or in a rough draft that is then not at all taken up into what is explicitly said or crafted. Thus a draft has been preserved for us that belongs to Hölderlin's elegy "Bread and Wine," specifically for its concluding strophe, a draft that even von Hellingrath failed to register.[5] Above lines 152–156 of the said elegy are found the words:

> nemlich zu Hauß ist der Geist
> Nicht im Anfang, nicht an der Quell. Ihn zehrt die Heimat.
> Kolonie liebt, und tapfer Vergessen der Geist.
> Unsere Blumen erfreun und die Schatten unserer Wälder
> Den Verschmachteten. Fast wär der Beseeler verbrandt.

> namely at home is spirit
> Not at the commencement, not at the source. The home consumes it.

---

5 Cf. Friedrich Beißner, *Hölderlins Übersetzungen aus dem Griechischen* (1933), 147.

Colony, and bold forgetting spirit loves.
Our flowers and the shades of our woods gladden
The one who languishes. The besouler would almost be scorched.

What is said here spans all relations of the essence of history of which Hölderlin knows. Yet what is said lets us clearly recognize only a few things, and this in a disconnected way. Taken at face value, it cannot be understood. Yet in the meantime we are no longer entirely unprepared. Here we must be content to highlight what relates to the concluding strophe of "Remembrance."

Spirit is "not at home" "at the source." This is why there is the need for the *passage* to the source. Why, namely at the beginning of history, is spirit not homely in the homeland? Because the latter "consumes." "Consuming" is a slow destruction and laying waste; something that uses up our energies, that is, withdraws them from their authentic use through mere expenditure, which is in itself inappropriate. In being expended, which from the outside always remains a being applied, our abilities are not freely determined from out of their essence and not released for the freedom of being authentically used. Their free use, by contrast, does not use up our ability but brings it rather into the streaming wealth of evolved usage. Consuming and consumption are found where the ability is not free to exercise that for which it is an ability.

In the beginning, the homeland is still closed off within itself, uncleared and unfree, and thus has not yet come to itself. This coming to "itself" demands a coming from something other. Going away to an other is the initial, as yet unappropriated distancing of the ability in relation to that for which it is an ability and within which it is to become free usage. Because the homeland demands a becoming homely, yet the latter, as a coming to oneself, must be a coming home, for this reason the spirit of the homeland itself demands the foreign from which alone a homecoming can proceed in any instance:

Kolonie liebt, und tapfer Vergessen der Geist.

Colony, and bold forgetting spirit loves.

The stay in the foreign and the learning of the foreign, not for the sake of the foreign, but for the sake of one's own, demands that enduring waiting that no longer thinks of one's own. Such absence of remembrance is not the forgetting that stems from indifference, but rather from the boldness of heart, which likewise remains certain of one's own that is coming.

The line "Colony, and bold forgetting spirit loves" is followed by:

Unsere Blumen erfreun und die Schatten unserer Wälder
Den Verschmachteten. Fast wäre der Beseeler verbrannt.

Our flowers and the shades of our woods gladden
The one who languishes. The besouler would almost be scorched.

Previously, the thought has been that spirit still resides in the foreign. In the meantime, without this being explicitly stated here, it has found the homeland again: it, the one who languishes, "the besouler," who would "almost be scorched." "The besouler" is the poet, the one in whose soul the thoughts of spirit quietly end, so as from the soul to be born to the word. The naming of the "besouler" says unequivocally that these lines everywhere refer to the being at home and not being at home, the going into the foreign and returning home of the poet.

In the foreign land, the heavenly fire is the element that is one's own. This threatens to scorch the poet, who has a different homeland that he seeks, so that he is entirely unable to learn the use of what is his own. For such learning cannot be accomplished in the realm of the indeterminate, as though it were merely the acquisition of an empty technique. Free use needs an inner relation to what is to be presented, that is, to the holy, for which the soil of the homeland must be consecrated.

Yet what the poet wants is "nothing mighty." "What" is summoned for the protection of what is "wanted" requires no extravagance: "Our flowers and the shades of our woods gladden"—nothing else. These are the gifts that help by virtue of simply blossoming and standing there, and that grant the favor for what is most difficult: to commence poetically with the commencement from out of the commencement, and that means, to ready the holidays for the festival.

For this, the attunement of the festive ground must remain awake; that which prevails in essence and once was, which attunes this fundamental attunement, must hold sway throughout the saying and hearing in the commemorative dialogue. The poet who has come home has not reproached the poets and companions of the foreign land; only it has now become clear and decided how everything inceptual has separated the own of the foreign and the own of the homely.

In the other Danube hymn, "At the Source of the Danube," Hölderlin says (IV, 160):

Ein unaufhörlich Lieben wars und ists.
Und wohl geschieden, aber darum denken
Wir aneinander doch, . . .

An unceasing loving it was and is.
And well separated, yet therefore we think
Of each other after all, . . .

Remembrance remains, and is itself attuned to "think" that which remains, if only this thinking, as the poet's thinking, has found its way into its own essence and has come into the free use of its own, that is, into the clarity of presentation.

Meanwhile the passage to one's own has begun. Unnoticed by the many, the poet has come home. His companions, however, have gone still further into the distance, sooner to find their way back. At such a time, when there is both sea voyage and unceasing loving and one's own seeking for one's own on the native soil of the homeland, there must also be found there for the first time "the clarity of presentation" for poetizing, that is, it must be poetized. What "remembrance" is in the articulated fullness of its essence becomes word:

> Es nehmet aber
> Und giebt Gedächtnis die See,
> Und die Lieb' auch heftet fleissig die Augen.
> Was bleibet aber, stiften die Dichter.

> Yet what takes
> And gives memory is the sea,
> And love too fixes with intensity our eyes.
> Yet what remains, the poets found.

The sea voyage leads off into the foreign. The sea "sublates" thinking of the homeland, because the colony-loving spirit loves "bold forgetting." However, as the sea takes our thinking back to the abandoned and at the same time still unappropriated homeland, it indeed first gives, within the foreign to which it leads as something foreign, a thinking ahead to the other of the foreign. That is one's own.

§65. The founding of the coming holy in the word

Likewise, love releases our view from the bonds of the contingent and transforms it into a view of the essence, one that "with intensity," that is, intentionally, is directed only toward the essential. That is the encountering of humans and gods: the bridal festival.

Yet even though the sea voyage and love, in their remembrance of what once was, already think ahead into that which is coming, still, taken by themselves and despite all effort and all intensity, they never satisfy what is entrusted to care. They prepare the while of equalized destiny, and yet do not ready for it the open realm within which it can be historical and grant a dwelling site to humans. The human being, however, "dwells poetically upon this Earth." The while is first readied when that which tarries in the while can become openly manifest and find the open realm for presentation.

In its inceptual coming, the holy must be said, become grounded in the word, bestowed as the word to the sons of the Earth, thus bringing their language back to the dialogue. Only in the word do love and deeds attain the ground of their essence. That which is coming inceptually, however, does not let itself be "brought together" in the manner of painters. The grounding bestowal of the inceptual is founding. Only the poets who have gone over the footbridge to the source are able to found. Because, however, at the source everything is inceptual, the essence of this poetizing must also first be poetized. Hölderlin has poetized the essence of the coming poets and enclosed everything in this one word:

Was bleibet aber, stiften die Dichter.

Yet what remains, the poets found.

What is poetized in the poem "Remembrance" is the essence and the essential time-space of a thinking that must remain unknown to every doctrine of thinking hitherto. Commemorative thinking thinks in the direction of the festival that once was, in thinking ahead to the coming festival. This remembrance that thinks back and thinks ahead, however, prior to both of these, thinks in the direction of what is fitting. Thinking directed toward what is fitting belongs to destiny. Such "thinking" belonging is the inceptual essence of remembrance.

To be able to found what remains, the poet himself must be one who remains; he must be capable of this one thing: to remain amid the many things that remain to be borne in the long time and to be said in song.

The Danube hymn "At the Source of the Danube" concludes as follows (IV, 161):

Darum, ihr Gütigen! umgebet mich leicht,
Damit ich bleiben möge, denn noch ist manches zu singen,
Jezt aber endiget, seeligweinend,
Wie eine Sage der Liebe,
Mir der Gesang, und so auch ist er
Mir, mit Erröthen, Erblassen,
Von Anfang her gegangen. Doch Alles geht so.

And so, you gracious ones! embrace me gently,
That I may remain, for much is still to be sung,

But now ends, in tears of bliss,
Like a saga of love,
For me the song, and so too has it
Gone for me, blushing, growing pale,
From the commencement. But everything goes that way.

Appendix

The Interpretive Structure for the Said Poems

September 1941

1. The interpretation of "Remembrance" provides the foundation and orientation, and the perspectives for all that follows.

The fundamental attunement of the thinking poet. Thanking.

2. In the interpretation of "Remembrance" itself, the elucidation of the first two strophes and the transition to the third are essential.

To be shown here: Hölderlin's thinking of history. Historicality and the festival. The poetic dwelling of humans. The encountering of humans and gods. The demigod. The poet.
The free use of one's own.
Grounding in the homely.
The necessity of preparation. Learning in the "dialogue."

3. Everywhere already point ahead to essential connections within the said poems.

Thus *before* the interpretation of these poems, that which has been founded, as founded in the hymns, must stand openly manifest within the time-space of its reign. Only thus can the word of interpretation become an appropriate one in its finer details.

EDITOR'S EPILOGUE

I.

In its form, the title of this volume does not correspond to Martin Heidegger's manuscript at the time it was written but rather to the label that he gave the folder to distinguish between this and the Hölderlin lecture course that follows (volume 53: *Hölderlin's Hymn "The Ister"*) in their subsequent use.

For the winter semester of 1941–1942, Heidegger had initially announced "Nietzsche's Metaphysics" as the title of his lecture course. In the rector's confirmation indicating a change (October 20, 1941), a new title is given: "Hölderlin's Hymns and German Metaphysics." This title has not hitherto been corroborated by a letter or section of manuscript in Heidegger's hand. The expression "German metaphysics" is not used in the lecture course.

The manuscript bears the title "Hölderlin's Hymns," as does that of the lecture course from the summer semester of 1942. This plurality presumably relates to the five hymns and fragments named at the beginning of the lecture course. The note offering a preview of the intent of the undertaking, and that is reproduced here as an appendix, also speaks of a plurality of poems to be interpreted in the given context. On German page 39, there is a mention of "the *second* poem we shall draw attention to"; the "Ister" lecture course too begins with a plurality: "several of Hölderlin's poetic works." Heidegger accordingly in these places still had his initial plan in view. The appendix also already maintains the foundational significance of "Remembrance" for the interpretation of all the envisaged poems. It is thus understandable that the endeavor to think what is poetized in "Remembrance" took up the entire lecture course of the winter semester of 1941–1942. The four other poems named at the outset are indeed touched upon, albeit very briefly. Thus, the simple title "Hölderlin's Hymns" would not indicate the actual content of the lecture course.

Given that "Remembrance" had been discussed in its foundational significance, Heidegger at the beginning of the "Ister" lecture course in the summer semester of 1942 may have continued to have the original plan in view. Perhaps he did not anticipate that "The Ister," the "*second* poem" whose interpretation was planned in 1941, would take up the entire duration of the lecture course. However things may stand in this regard, the identical title "Hölderlin's Hymns" in the manuscripts of "Remembrance" and "The Ister" must be acknowledged in order to be able to think through how the two lecture courses belong together in terms of the original plan. The fact that a more condensed elucidation of "Remembrance," sometimes borrowing from the lecture course, was written in August 1942 for the Hölderlin commemorative volume of 1943,[1] is also indicative of the foundational significance of the poem for Heidegger's Hölderlin interpretation noted here in the appendix.

Heidegger labeled the folders for the manuscripts with the added titles "Remembrance" and "The Ister," without recording these additional titles in the manuscripts. He provided one copy of the typewritten transcript of the second lecture course, prepared by Frau Vietta, with the title "M. H. / Hölderlin / The Ister" on a handwritten cover sheet. Whether this is to be regarded as a decision concerning the final title that was likewise not carried over into the manuscript, must remain an open question. Correspondingly, had the title "Hölderlin / Remembrance" been adopted for the present volume, it would have sounded too similar to the title of the elucidation given in the Hölderlin commemorative volume.

Since, moreover, the two lecture courses are being published in two separate volumes, it seemed appropriate to choose for the first lecture course the title that now appears: it maintains in modified form the title of the manuscript and the label of the folder, indicates the content precisely, is clearly distinguished from the title "Remembrance" of the elucidation, and at the same time is in keeping with volume 39 (*Hölderlin's Hymns "Germania" and "The Rhine"*).

II.

The lecture course was held for one hour at a time. The text is based on Heidegger's manuscript, as well as the few alterations and brief additions that he made in a typewritten manuscript prepared by his brother Fritz Heidegger. The manuscript consists of sixty-seven sheets, written on one side in horizontal folio format, numbered pages 1 through 64 (together with three inserted pages marked as a, b, c). In addition there are four

---

1 "Andenken," in: *Hölderlin. Gedenkschrift zu seinem 100. Todestag*, edited by Paul Kluckhohn (Tübingen, 1943), 267–324. [This refers to the essay "Andenken," also included in *Erläuterungen zu Hölderlins Dichtung* from the second edition onward (Frankfurt: Klostermann, 1951), 75–143. Translated as *Elucidations of Hölderlin's Poetry* by Keith Hoeller (Amherst, New York: Humanity Books, 2000), 101–173. —Trans.]

smaller sheets with "additional materials," bibliographical details, and the note reproduced as the appendix which (other than the remark "winter semester 1941–42" on page 1) bears the only date. On the left half of the pages is the running text, and on the right are written numerous insertions and new versions of deleted portions of the text, themselves often again altered, supplemented, and nestled within one another.

The separate manuscript of the Reviews, likewise written on one side in horizontal folio format, consists of nineteen sheets. The left and right sides of the pages are organized in the same way as those of the text of the lectures. The places in the text of the lectures where the Reviews were inserted are precisely marked by Heidegger; this is where they have in each case been integrated into the published text.

Collating the manuscripts and typewritten transcript revealed additions and corrections to the transcript. It further revealed that Heidegger presumably did not undertake any precise collation, for only a minority of the readings that deviate from the manuscript have been corrected by him in the transcript. Textual alterations (mostly making points more precise) and additions made in his own hand in the transcript have been retained. There are so few overall that one must say that he let the version that he wrote in 1941–1942 stand as definitive throughout. In keeping with the guidelines for the edition of the lecture courses, various marginal remarks containing, for example, references to "SS [summer semester] 1942," or notes remarking on particular connections, were not incorporated. The deletion of the beginnings of sentences with "And . . . ," of fillers, as well as the reordering of words, was carefully undertaken in accordance with Heidegger's guidelines; that is, not everywhere where such things occur, particularly not where beginning a sentence with "And . . ." clarifies an overarching link, or where deletions would disturb the rhythm of the text or of the sentence. The different way in which lines of verse are cited, sometimes excerpted as freely standing lines, sometimes integrated within the paragraphs of the interpretation, was everywhere reproduced. Considerably more paragraphs were introduced into the text than could be discerned in the manuscripts.

The manuscripts and transcript were not divided into sections by Heidegger himself. Only the title "Remembrance" marks the place where, following the Preliminary Considerations for the original overall plan (see the third and fourth paragraphs in section I above), the interpretation of this poem begins. This title, which corresponds to the thematic main part of the lecture course that was actually given, was left intact. Following the Preliminary Considerations, which extend to section 7, sections 8 through 10 may be regarded as a "second" series of preparations, as it were, which lead more closely and particularly to "Remembrance."

The division into preliminary considerations and four parts stems from the editor, as does the choice of section titles. With the aid of these titles the lecture course has been subdivided relatively rigorously; that is, this repeatedly gave rise to distinctly short sections of text. This was intended to accommodate as closely as possible Heidegger's demand for a clearly emerging form for the construction of the lecture course and for individual steps, including the overview provided by the table of contents.

III.

Attention may be drawn to the statement "The lecture course is only a pointing," which is added to the manuscript like a kind of motto. It is found there in square brackets, and was therefore perhaps not read out. One may further point out the restrained way in which Heidegger characterizes his own interpretation when in this course he calls his lectures "comments" [*Bemerkungen*] and in the "Ister" lecture course speaks of "remarks" [*Anmerkungen*]. (Similarly, an initial version of the title for the elucidation published in 1943 read: "Remarks on Hölderlin's Poem 'Remembrance.'") This cautious characterization of his own beginning, almost reticent in its choice of words, corresponds to the immediate proximity in which Hölderlin's poetizing struck Heidegger's thinking. That something happened thereby that demands to be carefully pondered was indeed seen quite early on already (for example, by Max Kommerell); however, it has as yet scarcely been brought to language in a manner that correctly approximates it. Heidegger's three Hölderlin lecture courses open the previously published *Elucidations of Hölderlin's Poetry* to new standards and perspectives of questioning, in accordance with the exceptional significance that the encounter with Hölderlin's poetizing has in his thinking.

I give my heartfelt thanks to Herr Dr. Hermann Heidegger and Herr Prof. Dr. Friedrich-Wilhelm von Herrmann for friendly and beneficial discussions on questions that arose in the course of my work, and also for assistance with literary, bibliographical, and documentary inquiries. For their attentive checking of the galley proofs I thank Frau Dr. Luise Michaelsen, Frau Dr. Gerda Utermöhlen, and Herr Prof. Dr. Walter Biemel.

Curd Ochwadt

TRANSLATORS' NOTES

[1.] The phrase "poetizes over and beyond" here translates the German verb *überdichten*, which conveys the sense of an excess that is poetized in the poet's word. The poet's word "overpoetizes" or "outpoetizes" the poet, we might say.

[2.] Heidegger here uses *gestoppt* as an instance of the "Americanization" of German.

[3.] This section presents particular difficulty for any attempt to translate it into English. In German, *das Wort* can mean either the individual word, regarded as an item of vocabulary, or it can mean "the word" in the sense of what is properly said or meant in and through particular words (as in "the Word of God"). In English, *the word* bears the same ambiguity. In German, however, these different senses are differently marked in the plural: when *das Wort* is intended in the first sense (as a grammatical unit), it is pluralized as *die Wörter*; when intended in the second sense (what is meant or intended), the plural is *die Worte*. English has no equivalent way of marking the distinction in the plural. Thus, in the present translation, we have for the most part resorted to simply rendering *die Worte* as "the word" while indicating the German plural noun in brackets. Where the plural "words" is used, it always refers to *die Wörter*, unless otherwise indicated.

[4.] The German here cites "the word" in both singular and plural: *Aber Sprache selbst gibt es nur, wo Worte sind, wo das Wort ist.*

[5.] This elegy is also known under the title *"Das Gasthaus"* ("The Guest House"), dedicated to the poet's friend Landauer.

[6.] The reference is to Austrian writer, poet, and painter Adalbert Stifter (1805–1868), also referred to in §36, and whose concept of "the gentle law" (*das sanfte Gesetz*) is outlined in the preface to his 1853 collection of stories, *Bunte Steine* (*Colorful Stones*).

[7.] "Coming to encounter" should here be understood not in the experiential sense of coming upon someone or something, but in the more literal sense of en-countering: coming toward, over and against, or counter to one another. This is suggested by the German *gegen* (toward, over against, counter) in *Entgegenkommen* ("coming to encounter"). Such reciprocity in coming to encounter is implicit within the "encountering," *Entgegnung*, which in German carries the sense of a reply or retort to an address.

[8.] *Dieses Stimmende durchstimmt und bestimmt alles als eine lautlose Stimme.* Heidegger here appeals to the relation of *stimmen* (to tune or attune), *durchstimmen* (to pervasively attune), and *bestimmen* (to determine, but also to call, in the sense of a calling or vocation: *die Bestimmung*) to the root *Stimme*, "voice."

[9.] *Trauerspiel* is another word for "tragedy," *Tragödie*, in German, but one that explicitly invokes *Trauer*, mourning or mournfulness. A *Trauerspiel* is thus literally a "mourning play." Notably, Heidegger uses both terms here, shifting from *Tragödie* to *Trauerspiel* so as to highlight the fundamental attunement of mourning. On the latter, see especially part 1, chapter 2, of Heidegger's first Hölderlin lecture course, *Hölderlins Hymnen "Germanien" und "Der Rhein."* Gesamtausgabe Bd. 39. Frankfurt: Klostermann, 1980. Translated as *Hölderlin's Hymns "Germania" and "The Rhine"* by William McNeill and Julia Ireland. Bloomington: Indiana University Press, 2014.

[10.] Both "fate" (*Schicksal*) and "that which is fitting" (*das Schickliche*) in German derive from the verb *schicken*, to send. The reflexive form *sich schicken* could mean to send or fit oneself. The difficulty of rendering the present section into English reflects the complexity with which Heidegger interweaves these senses of fitting and sending, senses that are also present in the term *Geschick* (destiny), which appears in the next section.

[11.] *"Träume sind Schäume."* The alliteration is lost in English.

[12.] "The real" here renders *das Wirkliche*. The Geman noun, however, derives from the verb *wirken*, to "effect" or to be actively "at work," as Heidegger proceeds to indicate. Moreover, *das Wirkliche* also means "the actual," particularly when contrasted with *das Mögliche*, "the possible," a contrast that Heidegger will shortly pursue. Thus, we have sometimes translated *das Wirkliche* as "the actually real" or "the actual and real," or simply "the actual," where this contrast with the possible is in play.

[13.] The German for "awe" here, *Scheu*, also means "shyness"—as in the friends' being "shy" to go to the source, in line 39 of the hymn. This sense of *Scheu* will be analysed by Heidegger in §58.

[14.] "Land of evening" and "land of morning" translate *Abendland* and *Morgenland* respectively. The *Abendland* or "land of evening" is the Western world or Occident; the *Morgenland* or "land of morning" is a designation for the East or Orient.

[15.] On *Gemüt* (conventionally translated as "mind"), the root *Mut* ("courage," but also "cheer"), and its many cognates, which Heidegger unfolds especially in this section and also in §54 (though *Großmut*, "magnanimity" and *Langmut*, "forbearance," are foreshadowed already in §44), see translators' note 16 in our translation of the lecture course that follows on "Remembrance," *Hölderlin's Hymn "The Ister."* Bloomington: Indiana University Press, 1996, 173.

GERMAN–ENGLISH GLOSSARY

die Abart — deviation

das Abendland; abendländisch — the Western world, Occident, land of evening; Western, Occidental

das Abwesen — privative essence

die Abwesenheit — absence

die Abwesung — absencing

ahnen — to intimate

das Andenken; das An-denken — remembrance; thoughtful remembrance, commemorative thinking

die Aneignung — appropriation

der Anfang; anfänglich — commencement, beginning; inceptual, of the commencement

der Anklang — intimation

ankommen; das Ankommen — to arrive; arrival

die Ankunft — arrival

die Anmut — gracefulness

der Anspruch — claim

die Anwesenheit — presence

die Anwesung — presencing

die Armut — poverty

aufbewahren — to safeguard

der Aufenthalt — stay, residence

der Aufgang — dawn

aufgeben; die Aufgabe — to give as a task; task

der Augenblick — moment

die Auseinandersetzung — confrontation

ausgleichen; der Ausgleich — to equalize; equalization

ausharren — to hold out, wait, wait out

die Auslegung — interpretation

bedenken — to ponder, ponder thoughtfully

behüten — to protect

der Bereich — realm

bergen; die Bergung — to shelter; sheltering

beseelen; der Beseeler — to besoul, animate; the besouler

besinnen; die Besinnung — to reflect; reflection

der Bestand — subsistence

bestimmen; die Bestimmung — to determine, define; vocation

bewahren; die Bewahrung — to preserve; preservation

der Bezirk — domain

bilden	to form
die Bindung	binding, being bound
bitten	to request
bleiben; das Bleiben	to remain; the remaining
das Bösartige	malice
das Böse	evil
brauchen	to need
das Brautfest	bridal festival
das Bündige	the bounded
die Darstellung	presentation
daselbst	thereat
das Dichtersein	being a poet
das Dichtertum	vocation of being a poet, poetic being
die Dichtung	poetizing, poetry
durchharren	to wait through
durchstimmen	to pervasively attune
die Edelmut	generosity
das Eigene; das Eigenste	what is proper, one's own; one's ownmost
eigentlich	authentic, proper
das Eigentum	property
die Eindeutigkeit; eindeutig	univocity, lack of ambiguity; univocal
der Einklang	accord
einsam	solitary
die Einzigkeit; einzig	singularity; singular
entgegenkommen	to encounter, come to encounter
die Entgegnung	encountering
die Entschiedenheit	decidedness
die Entsprechung	correspondence
die Entzückung	rapture
die Erde	Earth
sich ereignen	to transpire, come to pass
das Ereignis	event
erfahren	to experience
erharren	to await, withstand
erinnern; die Erinnerung	to recollect, recall; recollection
das Erlebnis	lived experience
erwarten	to expect
fahren; die Fahrt	to voyage; the voyage
feiern	to celebrate
der Feiertag	holiday
das Fest	festival
das Fremde	the foreign
die Freude	joy
die Freundschaft	friendship
der Fug	order, ordinance
die Fuge	jointure
fügen; sich fügen	to order, configure; to fit oneself

die Fügung	configuring
die Fügsamkeit	enjoining
der Gang	passage
der Gebrauch	use
das Gedächtnis	memory
das Gedenken	commemoration
das Gedicht	the poem
das Gedichtete	what is poetized
die Gefährten	companions
die Gegenwart	the present
gegenwartsnah	relevant to the present
das Gegenwesen	counter-essence
gehen	to go
das Geheimnis	mystery
zu Gehör bringen	to grant a hearing
der Geist	spirit
das Geläufige; geläufig	what is customary; accustomed
die Geschichte; geschichtlich	history; historical
das Geschick	destiny
das Geschwätz	chatter
das Gespräch	dialogue, the dialogue
gestehen; die Geständnis	to admit; admittance
gewähren	to grant
das Gewesene	what once was
der Glanz	radiance
die Gleichmut	equanamity
das Göttliche	the divine
das Griechenland	Greece, the land of the Greeks
das Griechentum	the Greek world
die Großmut	magnanimity
grüßen; der Gruß	to greet; the greeting
die Gunst	favor
die Haltung	disposition, stance
handeln	to act
harren	to wait
das Heilige	the holy
die Heimat	the homeland
heimatlich	of the homeland
heimisch	at home, homely, native
das Heimischwerden	coming to be at home
die Heimkehr; Heimkunft	the return home
die Herkunft	provenance
hindenken	thinking in the direction of, thinking toward
der Hinweis	pointer, hint
die Historie; historisch	historiography; historiographical
das Hochgemute	cheerfulness
horchen	to hearken
hören	to hear, listen

das Innige; innig	the intimate; intimate
die Innigkeit	intimacy
die Inständigkeit	steadfast insistence
die Irre	errancy
kommen; das Kommende	to come; what is coming
die Klarheit	clarity
die Kunde	tidings
künftig	futural
die Langmut	forbearance
die Loslassung	releasing
lauten	to sound
das Meer	ocean
die Meerfahrt	ocean voyage
das Menschentum	humankind
das Mitdichten	poetizing accompaniment
das Mitgebrachte	what is brought with
mitgehen	to go with
das Mitsein	being-with
mitwollen	shared willing
das Mögliche	the possible
das Morgenland	land of morning, Orient
die Mut	cheer, courage
nachdenken	to ponder, to think, to give careful thought
das Nichtseiende	the nonexistent
die Not	exigency, need, urgency, distress
die Nüchternheit	soberness
öffnen; das Offene	to open up; the open realm
die Opfermut	self-sacrifice
der Ort	locale
poetisch	poetical, poetological
die Quelle	source
rechnen	to calculate, to account, to reckon
das Rechte	what is right
der Reichtum	abundance, wealth
retten	to rescue
die Ruhe	restfulness, rest, peace, repose
sagen	to say, tell
die Sanftmut	gentleness
scheinen	to shine, to radiate
schenken; die Schenkung	to bestow; bestowal

German	English
die Scheu	awe, shyness
sich schicken	to fit, to fittingly send oneself
das Schickliche	what is fitting
das Schicksal	fate
schweben	to hover, oscillate
schweigen	to be silent
schwingen	to oscillate, resonate
das Schwerste	what is most difficult
die See	the sea
die Seele	soul
sein; seyn	being; beyng
das Sinnbild	sensuous image
die Sprache	language
das Sprachgebilde	linguistic constuction
der Steg	footbridge
stiften	to found
die Stimmung	attunement
die Tragödie	tragedy
die Trauer	mourning, mournfulness
das Trauerspiel	mourning play, tragedy
der Traum; das Traumhafte	dream; that which is dreamlike
überdichten	to poetize over and beyond
der Übergang	passing over, transition
überschwingen	to resonate over beyond
der Umkreis	ambit, sphere
das Ungesagte	the unsaid
ungeschichtlich	unhistorical
ungewöhnlich	inhabitual
unheimlich	uncanny
unscheinbar	improbable
der Untergang	downgoing, descent
untergehen	to go down, descend
das Unwesen	corrupted essence
das Unwirkliche	the unreal
der Ursprung; ursprünglich	origin; originary, primordial
das Vaterland	fatherland
verbergen	to conceal
das Verborgene	that which is concealed
verbürgen	to guarantee
vergänglich	transitory
das Vergehen	dissolution, passing away
das Verhalten	comportment
verhüllen	to veil
verlassen	to abandon
vernehmen	to apprehend
die Verrechnung	calculative accounting

verschlossen	hidden
verschweigen	to keep silent
versetzen	to transpose
die Versöhnung	reconciliation
verweilen	to tarry
die Vieldeutigkeit	multiplicity of meaning, polysemy
vorbereiten	to prepare
der Vorgang	process
vorhanden	present at hand, at hand
die Vorliebe	predilection
die Vorstellung	representation, vision
die Vorzeit	the time before
wagen	to venture
das Wahre; die Wahrheit	the true; truth
walten	to prevail, to reign
die Wanderung	journey
warten	to wait
der Weg	path
wegwesen	to prevail as away
die Weile	the while
werden	to become, come to be
wesen	to prevail in being, to prevail in essence, to presence
das Wesen	essence, essential prevailing
das Wesentliche	the essential, what is essential
die Wiederholung	review
willkürlich	arbitrary
winken	to beckon
wirken	to effect
das Wissen	knowing, knowledge
die Wohnstatt	site of dwelling
wollen	to will, to desire
das Wort	the word
die Worte	words (things said)
die Wörter	words (grammatical units)
zögern; die Zögerung	to hesitate; hesitation
das Zudenkende	that which is to be thought
das Zu-erschweigende	that which is to be kept silent
die Zugehörigkeit	belonging
das Zugewiesene	what is assigned
zurückbleiben	to remain behind
das Zu-sagende	that which is to be said
der Zusammenhang	connection, cohesion, context
die Zwiesprache	dialogue

ENGLISH–GERMAN GLOSSARY

to abandon	verlassen
absence	die Abwesenheit, das Fehlen, das Ausbleiben
absencing	die Abwesung
abundance	der Reichtum
accord	der Einklang
to account	rechnen
accustomed	geläufig
to act	handeln
to admit; admittance	gestehen; die Geständnis
ambit	der Umkreis
to animate	beseelen
to apprehend	vernehmen
appropriation	die Aneignung
arbitrary	willkürlich
arrival	das Ankommen, die Ankunft
to arrive	ankommen
what is assigned	das Zugewiesene
attunement	die Stimmung
to await	erharren
awe	die Scheu
authentic	eigentlich
to beckon	winken
beginning	der Beginn
to become	werden
being; beyng	sein; seyn
being a poet	das Dichtersein
being-with	das Mitsein
to prevail in being	wesen
belonging	die Zugehörigkeit
to besoul	beseelen
to bestow; bestowal	schenken; die Schenkung
binding, being bound	die Bindung
what is brought with	das Mitgebrachte
to calculate	rechnen
calculative accounting	die Verrechnung
to celebrate	feiern
chatter	das Geschwätz

cheer	die Mut
cheerfulness	das Hochgemute
claim	der Anspruch
clarity	die Klarheit
cohesion	der Zusammenhang
to come; what is coming	kommen; das Kommende
to come to be	werden
to come to pass	sich ereignen
commencement; of the commencement	der Anfang; anfänglich
commemoration	das Gedenken
commemorative thinking	das An-denken
companions	die Gefährten
comportment	das Verhalten
to conceal	verbergen
that which is concealed	das Verborgene
to configure; configuring	fügen; die Fügung
confrontation	die Auseinandersetzung
connection, context	der Zusammenhang
correspondence	die Entsprechung
corrupted essence	das Unwesen
courage	die Mut
what is customary	das Geläufige
counteressence	das Gegenwesen
dawn	der Aufgang
decidedness	die Entschiedenheit
to define	bestimmen
to descend	untergehen
to desire	wollen
destiny	das Geschick
to determine	bestimmen
deviation	die Abart
dialogue	das Gespräch, die Zwiesprache
what is most difficult	das Schwerste
disposition	die Haltung
dissolution	das Vergehen
distress	die Not
the divine	das Göttliche
domain	der Bezirk
to go down; downgoing	untergehen; der Untergang
dream; that which is dreamlike	der Traum; das Traumhafte
site of dwelling	die Wohnstatt
Earth	die Erde
to effect	wirken
to encounter, come to encounter	entgegenkommen
encountering	die Entgegnung
enjoining	die Fügsamkeit

to equalize; equalization	ausgleichen; der Ausgleich
equanimity	die Gleichmut
errancy	die Irre
essence, essential prevailing	das Wesen
the essential, what is essential	das Wesentliche
to prevail in essence	wesen
event	das Ereignis
evil	das Böse
exigency	die Not
to expect	erwarten
favor	die Gunst
fate	das Schicksal
fatherland	das Vaterland
festival	das Fest
to fit oneself	sich fügen
to fit, to fittingly send oneself	sich schicken
what is fitting	das Schickliche
footbridge	der Steg
forbearance	die Langmut
the foreign	das Fremde
to form	bilden
to found	stiften
friendship	die Freundschaft
futural	künftig
generosity	die Edelmut
gentleness	die Sanftmut
to go	gehen
to go with	mitgehen
to grant	gewähren
gracefulness	die Anmut
Greece, the land of the Greeks	das Griechenland
the Greek world	das Griechentum
to greet; the greeting	grüßen; der Gruß
to guarantee, ensure	verbürgen
to hear	hören
to grant a hearing	zu Gehör bringen
to hearken	horchen
to hesitate; hesitation	zögern; die Zögerung
hidden	verschlossen
hint	der Hinweis
historiography; historiographical	die Historie; historisch
history; historical	die Geschichte; geschichtlich
to hold out	ausharren
holiday	der Feiertag
the holy	das Heilige
at home, homely	heimisch

coming to be at home	das Heimischwerden
homeland	die Heimat
of the homeland	heimatlich
to hover	schweben
humankind	das Menschentum
improbable	unscheinbar
inceptual	anfänglich
inhabitual	ungewöhnlich
interpretation	die Auslegung
intimacy	die Innigkeit
the intimate; intimate	das Innige; innig
to intimate	ahnen
intimation	der Anklang
jointure	die Fuge
journey	die Wanderung
joy	die Freude
knowing, knowledge	das Wissen
lack of ambiguity	die Eindeutigkeit
land of evening	das Abendland
land of morning	das Morgenland
language	die Sprache
leeway	der Spielraum
linguistic construction	das Sprachgebilde
to listen	hören
lived experience	das Erlebnis
locale	der Ort
magnanimity	die Großmut
malice	das Bösartige
memory	das Gedächtnis
moment	der Augenblick
mourning, mournfulness	die Trauer
mourning play	das Trauerspiel
multiplicity of meaning	die Vieldeutigkeit
mystery	das Geheimnis
native	heimisch
to need	brauchen
need	die Not
the nonexistent	das Nichtseiende
ocean	das Meer
ocean voyage	die Meerfahrt
the Occident; Occidental	das Abendland; abendländisch
what is one's own; one's ownmost	das Eigene; das Eigenste

to open up; open realm	öffnen; das Offene
to order, configure; order, ordinance	fügen; der Fug
origin; originary, primordial	der Ursprung; ursprünglich
to oscillate	schweben, schwingen
passage	der Gang
passing away	das Vergehen
passing over	der Übergang
path	der Weg
peace	die Ruhe
to pervasively attune	durchstimmen
poem	das Gedicht
poetical, poetological	poetisch
poetic being	das Dichtertum
to poetize over and beyond	überdichten
poetizing, poetry	die Dichtung
poetizing accompaniment	das Mitdichten
what is poetized, that which is poetized	das Gedichtete
pointer	der Hinweis
polysemy	die Vieldeutigkeit
to ponder	nachdenken
to ponder, to ponder thoughtfully	bedenken
the possible	das Mögliche
poverty	die Armut
predilection	die Vorliebe
to prepare	vorbereiten
to presence	wesen
presence	die Anwesenheit
presencing	die Anwesung
the present	die Gegenwart
relevant to the present	gegenwartsnah
present at hand	vorhanden
presentation, setting forth	die Darstellung
to preserve; preservation	bewahren; die Bewahrung
to prevail	walten
to prevail as away	wegwesen
privative essence	das Abwesen
process	der Vorgang
what is proper	das Eigene
property	das Eigentum
to protect	behüten
provenance	die Herkunft
radiance	der Glanz
to radiate	scheinen
rapture	die Entzückung
realm	der Bereich
to reckon	rechnen

to recollect, recall; recollection	erinnern; die Erinnerung
reconciliation	die Versöhnung
to reflect; reflection	besinnen; die Besinnung
to reign	walten
releasing	die Loslassung
to remain behind	zurückbleiben
to remain; the remaining	bleiben; das Bleiben
remembrance; thoughtful remembrance	das Andenken; das An-denken
repose	die Ruhe
representation	die Vorstellung
to request	bitten
to rescue	retten
residence	der Aufenthalt
rest, restfulness	die Ruhe
to resonate	schwingen
to resonate over and beyond	überschwingen
return home	die Heimkehr, die Heimkunft
review	die Wiederholung
what is right	das Rechte
to safeguard	aufbewahren
that which is to be said	das Zu-sagende
to say	sagen
sea	die See
self-sacrifice	die Opfermut
sensuous image	das Sinnbild
shared willing	mitwollen
to shelter; shelter	bergen; die Bergung
to shine	scheinen
shyness	die Scheu
singularity; singular	die Einzigkeit; einzig
to be silent	schweigen
to keep silent	verschweigen
that which is to be kept silent	das Zu-erschweigende
soberness, sobriety	die Nüchternheit
solitary	einsam
soul	die Seele
to sound	lauten
source	die Quelle
sphere	der Umkreis
spirit	der Geist
stance	die Haltung
stay	der Aufenthalt
steadfast insistence	die Inständigkeit
subsistence	der Bestand
to give as a task; task	aufgeben; die Aufgabe
to tarry	verweilen

to tell	sagen
thereat	daselbst
to think, to give careful thought	nachdenken
thinking in the direction of, thinking toward	hindenken
that which is be thought	das Zudenkende
tidings	die Kunde
the time before	die Vorzeit
tragedy	die Tragödie
transitory	vergänglich
to transpire	sich ereignen
transition	der Übergang
to transpose	versetzen
the true	das Wahre
truth	die Wahrheit
uncanny	unheimlich
unhistorical	ungeschichtlich
the unreal	das Unwirkliche
univocity; univocal	die Eindeutigkeit; eindeutig
the unsaid	das Ungesagte
urgency	die Not
use	der Gebrauch
to veil	verhüllen
to venture	wagen
vision	die Vorstellung
vocation	die Bestimmung
vocation of being a poet	das Dichtertum
to voyage; voyage	fahren; die Fahrt
to wait	ausharren, harren, warten
to wait out	ausharren
to wait through	durchharren
what once was	das Gewesene
wealth	der Reichtum
wedding festival	das Brautfest
Western, Occidental	abendländisch
the Western world	das Abendland
while	die Weile
to will	wollen
to withstand	erharren
the word	das Wort (intended meaning), die Worte (things said)
words	die Wörter (grammatical units)